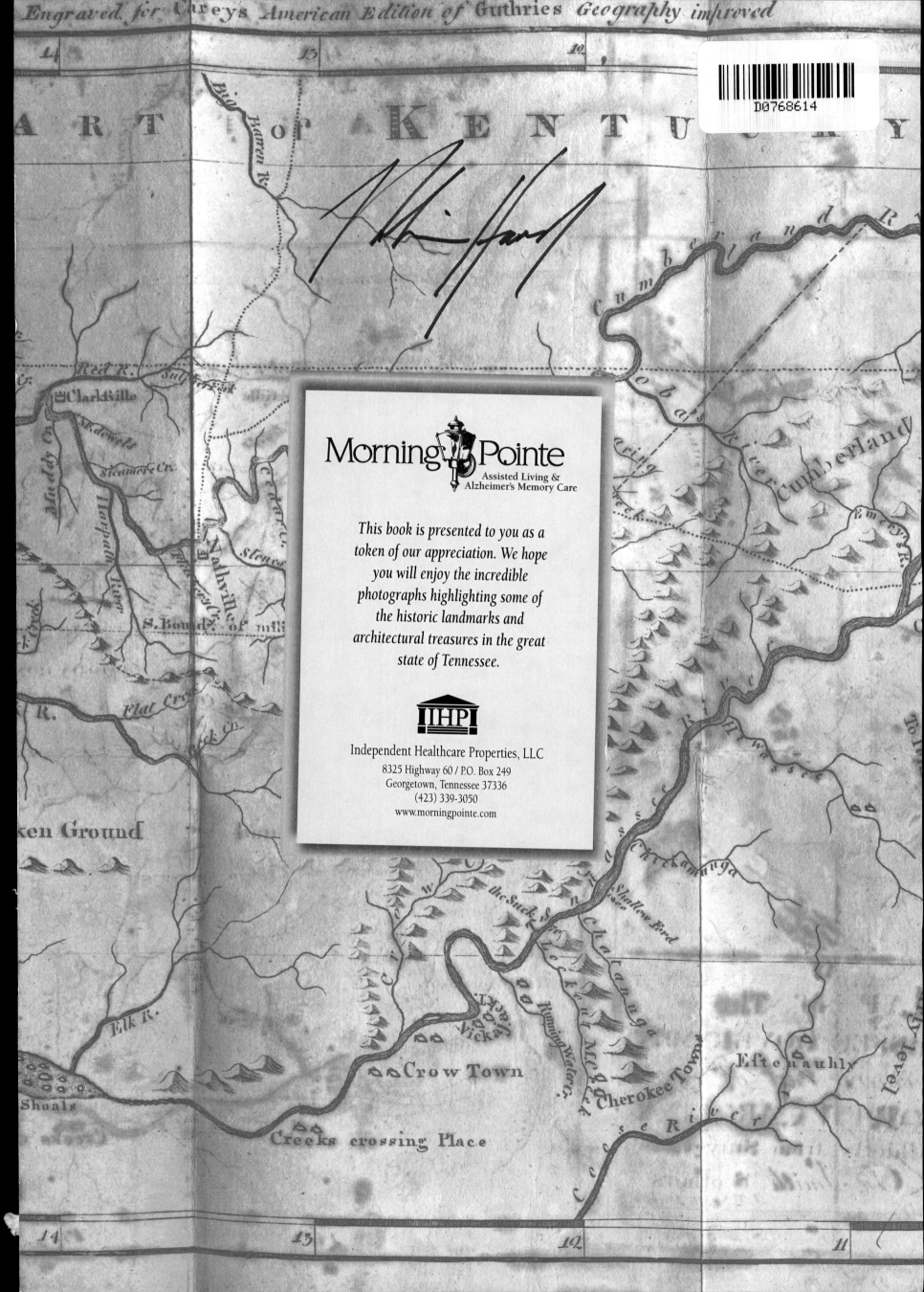

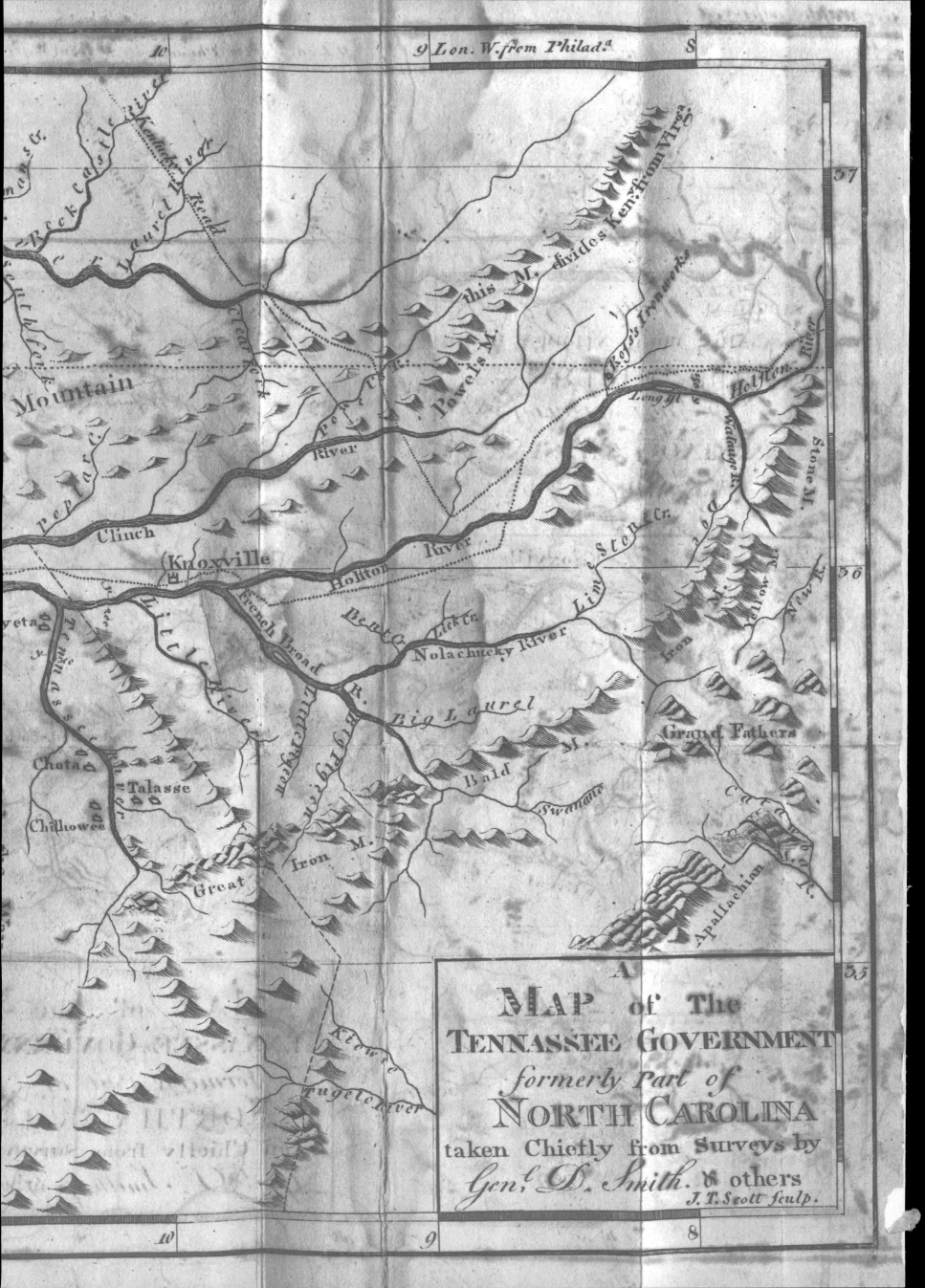

A
MAP of The
TENNASSEE GOVERNMENT
formerly Part of
NORTH CAROLINA
taken Chiefly from Surveys by
Genl. D. Smith & others
J. T. Scott sculp.

This book is made possible through the generous support of our sponsors:

 **FIRST TENNESSEE.**
powering your dreams

 **CHP** MTSU Center for Historic Preservation
History · Education · Architecture

 **IHP**
Independent Healthcare Properties, LLC

 Morning Pointe
Assisted Living & Alzheimer's Memory Care

U.S. XPRESS ENTERPRISES, INC.

 the **FACTORY at FRANKLIN**

 **REPUBLIC PARKING SYSTEM**

 **FRANKLIN REALTORS INC**

GILLHAM FOUNDATION
Fred and Kelli Gillham

 **TENNESSEE**
DEPARTMENT OF ECONOMIC & COMMUNITY DEVELOPMENT

 **TENNESSEE**
★ THE STAGE IS SET FOR YOU ★
tnvacation.com

Tennessee Preservation Trust

Historic TENNESSEE

Text by James A. Crutchfield
Photography by Robin Hood

GRANDIN HOOD
Publishers

Published by:
Grandin Hood Publishers
1101 West Main Street
Franklin, Tennessee 37064
www.grandinhood.com

Designed by Robertson Design, Inc.,
    Franklin, Tennessee
Digital retouching by Lauren Hood,
    Franklin, Tennessee
Proofreading by: Lisa Grimenstein,
    Columbia, Tennessee
Printed in China through Asia Pacific
    Offset, Inc.

ISBN: 0-9771281-7-2

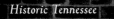

St. John's Episcopal Church near
Mt. Pleasant

Previous spread: John Oliver Cabin,
homeplace of Cades Cove's first
settlers, John and Lurena Oliver

—•— Contents —•—

HISTORIC TENNESSEE

in order of presentation

⊷ Contents ⊶

HISTORIC TENNESSEE ENCORE

in order of presentation

⸺ ♦ ▸ ⸺

⸺ *Acknowledgments* ⸺

The publisher wishes to acknowledge the generous contribution of the following individuals who assisted with the publication of *HISTORIC TENNESSEE*. Foremost among this group is the Book Committee who provided clear focus and a historically accurate compass for the book's content. The committee included Patrick McIntyre who has championed this project since its earliest inception many years ago, Carroll Van West, whose continuing vision is a mantra for the importance of historic preservation to Tennesseans, and Dan Brown, immediate past executive director of the Tennessee Preservation Trust who instilled his passion for diversity and architectural accuracy within these pages. We also thank James A. Hoobler, Curator, Tennessee State Museum, for making portraits, artifacts, and archival photographs from the Museum's collection available for illustrating many of the site profiles.

A special salute goes to Chairman Greg Vital and Vice Chairman Ernie Bacon of the Tennessee Preservation Trust for their leadership with the project and for their untiring efforts in securing the Underwriters for the book. And, most importantly, we extend a special thanks to the Underwriting Partners for their unstinting generosity in making this book possible.

Archival Photo Credits

Unless otherwise credited herein, archival photographs were provided by the Tennessee State Museum. Additional credits in order of appearance: Main Street Jonesboro - Anne Mason, Jonesboro Heritage Alliance; Crockett Birthplace - Tennessee State Library and Archives; President Andrew Johnson Home - Kendra Hinkle; Rogersville - George Webb, Jr. Collection; Blount Mansion - Nancy Kelly, President, and Sarah Rainwater; Ramsey House - Sandra Gammon, Director; Sam Houston Schoolhouse - Bob Bell, Manager; Cades Cove - Annette Hartigan, Librarian, Great Smoky Mountains National Park; Niota Depot - Fred Underdown, McMinn County Historical Association; Adolph Ochs Building - Greg Vital and Becky Browder, Dome Building Realty Partners; Tivoli Theatre - David Johnson, Deputy Administrator, and Donna Landry, Marketing Coordinator, Tivoli/Memorial Auditorium, and Judy Serna, In Circle Flight Design; Rugby Village - Barbara Stagg and George Zepp, Historic Rugby; Cairo Rosenwald School - Velma Brinkley; Sam Davis Home - Anita Teague, Executive Director, Sam Davis Memorial Association; The Hermitage - Tony Guzzi, Curator; Tulip Grove - Tony Guzzi, Curator; Tennessee State Capitol - Walter T. Durham; Fisk Jubilee Hall - Greg Bryant, Public Relations, Fisk University; Ryman Auditorium - Brenda Colladay, Museum Curator, Grand Ole Opry; Belle Meade - Alton Kelly, Executive Director; Belmont Mansion - Mark Brown, Executive Director; Travellers Rest - Brian Allison, Curator; Natchez Trace - James A. Crutchfield; Carnton Plantation - Eric Jacobson, Historian; Carter House - Eric Jacobson, Historian; Homestead Manor - Thomas Cartwright, Greg Biggs, and Rick Warwick; President James K. Polk Home - John Holtzapple, Executive Director; Hamilton Place - Fred Gillham; Beale Street Historic District - John Doyle, Executive Director, Memphis Rock 'n' Soul Museum, and Richard M. Raichelson; Memphis Cotton Exchange and Steamboat Wharf - Carol Perel, Executive Director, Cotton Exchange Museum: Encore Site Profile: Wynnewood - Jed DeKalb, Director, State of Tennessee Photographic Services.

⸺ ♦ ▸ ⸺

Preface

Traveling the roads of Tennessee, one is astonished by the accelerated pace of architectural preservation in our state and country, growing from the early champions of patriotic monuments into the current broad-based groundswell of public support. It is a rekindling of interest in our past as the foundation for the future and a realization of how important history and its structures can be in helping us define our communities. Interest in the rich form, decoration, and detail of historical structures is a reaction to the public's boredom with mass-produced architecture of big-box strip malls and suburbia.

This book's story is about historic architecture and treasured sites in Tennessee. The collection is in no way a comprehensive presentation of all Tennessee's historic buildings, but an effort to expand traditional perspectives of historic sites and to engage a broader segment of the public.

The treasures that have been photographed include a diverse collection of archeological, Native American, African-American, early industrial, and residential sites, in addition to the traditional architectural canon. This project has included sites thousands of years old as well as modern sites spanning the three centuries of growth in Tennessee. From Rocky Mount in Piney Flats to the Steamboat Wharf on the banks of the Mississippi River in Memphis, the sites are presented east to west, in a mirror of our state's history and exemplify this broadened perspective on historic places.

The Tennessee Preservation Trust promotes the preservation of Tennessee's diverse historical resources. The organization has been a statewide leader in conjunction with the National Trust for Historic Preservation in the preservation of historic places since the early 1980s and is its official statewide partner.

Since 2001, Tennessee Preservation Trust has powerfully advocated for many endangered sites through its annual "Ten Most Endangered Historic Sites in Tennessee." Its "Ten in Tennessee" list identifies ten sites each year that are of exceptional historical importance and may be endangered in a variety of ways, such as neglect, development, or demolition. This list also serves as a catalyst to save many of these properties and provides the basis of much of its work in advocacy and preservation efforts.

For several reasons, this book concentrates on the vast resources and numerous styles of historic structures in Tennessee from early settlers' cabins to Greek Revival mansions, and from classic theaters to public buildings. Fortunately, builders turn to indigenous designs and readily available materials, producing structures as varied as the terrain and climate. Located in a variety of settings, both urban and rural, they were constructed with forms, materials, and architecture compatible with their environment.

The richness and diversity of the architecture provides a wealth of cultural resources. Current threats from overuse, neglect, and, in some cases, abandonment are compelling reasons for the public to be aware of the dangers facing the structures that we call Tennessee's historical treasures. Collaborative efforts among the public, local and state governments, the educational community, and the private sector have resulted in a variety of buildings and structures being preserved for future generations throughout Tennessee.

We owe a special debt of gratitude to Patrick McIntyre, the state historic preservation officer and executive director of the Tennessee Historical Commission. The Tennessee Historical Commission is the state's premier partner for Tennessee Preservation Trust's yearly Statewide Preservation Conference and Main Street Summit. Our organization is also grateful to Dr. Carroll Van West, the executive director of the Middle Tennessee State University's Center for Historic Preservation. Besides partnering as an underwriter for this book, Dr. West and the Center have partnered with our organization and have provided support for many years. Both of these individuals have generously served on the book's site selection committee.

I personally want to thank the board of directors of the Tennessee Preservation Trust for their support of this project and their tireless volunteer effort, especially Ernie Bacon and Pam Lewis for their selfless efforts to obtain underwriters and to spread the message of Tennessee's resources and treasured sites across the state. Most importantly, we are deeply indebted to our generous underwriters who through their enlightened support of this project are not only supporting us as we complete our mission, but are expanding the message of historic preservation. Lastly, we are grateful to our publisher and Pulitzer Prize-winning photographer, Robin Hood, whose insight and keen eye have shared the message of preservation through his talent and love of history and preservation for posterity's sake. In *Historic Tennessee*, you will see some of Robin Hood's most impressive photographs to date.

Greg A. Vital, Chairman
Tennessee Preservation Trust

— Mission Statement —

I am honored to be a part of this book featuring the remarkable photography of Robin Hood, whose compelling images highlight some of the most notable historic places in Tennessee. This wonderful assemblage is comprehensive but by no means exhaustive, and the sites in this publication are a broad sampling of some of the fantastic resources that serve as tangible links to the rich and diverse heritage of our state.

It is worth noting with pride that Tennessee claims the nation's second oldest organized preservation group, the Ladies' Hermitage Association, established in 1889. Today our state's historic preservation efforts continue to be well-served by organizations such as the Tennessee Preservation Trust (TPT), its members and affiliated groups, and the public and private stewards of the sites featured in this book. First chartered as the Tennessee Heritage Alliance in 1982, TPT works through advocacy to unite individuals and local and regional organizations and fosters the protection of the state's irreplaceable historic buildings, sites, and neighborhoods. The organization also serves as a guiding force for preservation education through the Statewide Preservation Conference, held each year in a different community. Since 2001, TPT's annual endangered list, "Ten in Tennessee," has brought needed attention to threatened historic properties, ranging from the circa 1000 AD Chucalissa Archaeological Site in Memphis, to the 1854 Niota Depot, to the circa 1929 Alvin York Institute in Jamestown.

The work of historic preservation is not only important but is in many ways critical to community sustainability. Every town has areas of new development that look no different from any other town in America, but the special inheritance provided by a community's historic assets help imbue it with a sense of identity and pride. Treasured landmarks are often cornerstones for the local economy, bringing in visitors and spurring the revitalization of the area. Old buildings are often remarkably adaptable to new uses, with former factories becoming loft apartments and past department stores transforming into artists' studios. Studies consistently show that properties in designated historic districts

---

*The special inheritance provided by a community's historic assets
help imbue it with a sense of identity and pride.*

typically appreciate at a higher rate than those in other types of neighborhoods. Heritage supporters are also quick to point out the substantial environmental benefits of reusing historic buildings, which usually contain construction materials superior to those found today, noting that "old buildings are the greenest buildings of all."

As one looks through these pages, it is worth remembering that our time-honored places do not save themselves. As the late photographer Richard Nickel wryly observed, "great architecture has only two natural enemies—water and stupid men." Virtually every property featured in this book, including the Ryman Auditorium and the Tennessee State Capitol, has been threatened at one point or another, by recurring maintenance needs if not by the prospect of a looming wrecking ball. Therefore, we must never take for granted that a restored site is protected forever, because keeping a property takes both a renewed commitment of time and resources every few years. My hope is that this book will serve both as a testament to all who have protected our historic places in the past, and as a call to each of us now and in the future to do all we can to see that the valued historic places of Tennessee remain a vibrant part of our ever-changing world.

E. Patrick McIntyre Jr., Executive Director
Tennessee Historical Commission

— Foreword —

TENNESSEE'S PHOTOGRAPHER LAUREATE

We Tennesseans love stories about ourselves. No one tells these stories better than the improbably named photographer, Robin Hood. I first met Robin in 1978 while I was walking 1,000 miles across our state to become its governor, and Robin was a Pulitzer Prize-winning photographer for the Chattanooga Free Press. Robin walked along with me for miles taking many pictures, including one of me coming out of an outhouse in Grassy Cove in Cumberland County. When I became governor I asked him to be Tennessee's director of photography.

The first project on which Robin and I worked together was *The Tennesseans*, a retrospective of my walk across the state. Robin and his camera revisited, among others, Levi Collins in Caryville, the Walking Horse Celebration in Shelbyville, and N.T. Richardson's store in Grand Junction. A few years later, as Tennessee became the favorite destination for Japanese manufacturing companies, I asked Robin to create the story of this new and unlikely relationship between the Japanese and Tennesseans. Robin's book, *Friends*, shows what a state and country, so seemingly different, have in common, such as red maples and boy scouts, mountain cabins and oversized wrestlers, mountain mist and baseball fans. For the last twenty years, now in private business, Robin and his associates have produced book after remarkable book telling Tennessee's story in photographs.

This latest volume, *Historic Tennessee*, tells the story of our state through its historic structures. These stories touch many of us in personal ways. For example, the end of the Revolutionary War in 1783 unleashed a stream of land-hungry settlers into the Nolichucky settlements in what is now northeastern Tennessee. One of these pioneers, 19-year-old Francis Alexander Ramsey, walked from Pennsylvania down the Shenandoah Valley to live with his uncle, John Alexander,

*Francis Alexander Ramsey settled about ten miles out of town,
near the confluence of the French Broad and Holston Rivers,
in an area called Swan Pond, named for a small lake
that teemed with swans, geese, ducks, and other waterfowl.*

who had already settled in Limestone. In 1797, Francis, who was a surveyor, wandered on down to the Forks of the Holston and French Broad Rivers where he built the first stone house in Knox County. When John Alexander became blind in 1808, Francis returned the earlier hospitality by inviting his uncle to come live with him in that stone house. John, my seventh generation grandfather, soon died and was buried at the Ramsey House, one of the structures featured in this book. One son of Francis, J.G.M. Ramsey, was Tennessee's most renowned early historian. Another became the first elected mayor of Knoxville.

When I was governor, I designated a poet laureate and a state historian. I realize now that I overlooked something. I am sure that all who enjoy these photographs and stories and the wonderful books that have come before will not mind if, retroactively, I hereby designate Robin Hood as Tennessee's photographer laureate.

Lamar Alexander
United States Senator

⟶ Introduction ⟵

SPECIAL PLACES FROM OUR PAST FOR OUR FUTURE

Stretching from the Appalachian highlands to river bottoms of the mighty Mississippi, Tennessee is a beautiful, diverse, meaningful landscape, a land of hundreds if not thousands of special places that define our sense of place, of identity, and of history. No matter how small or large, how grandiose or plain, how early or late, these special places are doors into the stories of Tennessee, stories that amuse, inspire, and teach about our successes and our faults.

Reading this landscape of special places is not easy. This exciting new book, *Historic Tennessee*, explores over fifty historic properties. Each has a story to contribute to our understanding and appreciation of Tennessee's past. We preserve our landmarks, in part, for how they look—good architecture is always an inspiration. But as we preserve that Greek Revival-style column, that Federal-style doorway, or that Queen Anne-style turret, we also save a place that has a deeper resonance of meaning among its owners and the community that nurtures it.

Historic Tennessee cannot cover every special place; the timeline is too short and the accomplishments are too many. But within the outline of this book, we can see the patterns that have shaped our state's architectural and historical legacies.

The long history of Native Americans shaping their lives and the landscape of Tennessee is best understood by digging the clues out of the ground, like past explorations at Townsend in Blount County, at Brown's Creek in Davidson County, and at Chucalissa in Shelby County. The first settlers of Tennessee, however, also left huge structures that commanded views of the landscape for miles around. Visit Pinson Mounds in Madison County and hike to the top of Saul's Mound—equal to a seven-story building—and you grasp the flatness and richness of the Madison County landscape. Imagine the ceremonies that took place atop that mound or how it allowed tracking of herds of bison and elk that once roamed the land.

A vivid imagination also enlivens visits to our many frontier-era homes. Sitting quietly along the Nolichucky River is a reconstructed one-room log cabin, no bigger than a corn crib, that in its utter functionality says nothing, but at the same time proclaims history as a house type in which thousands of pioneers and their African-American slaves lived. From this cabin on the

---

Nolichucky, however, was born one of the most famous Tennessee heroes, David Crockett. As he grew up in the wilds of Greene and Washington counties, he encountered many homes just like his, mostly constructed of log, typically one room. Those with larger families often just added rooms. If the exterior chimney was left in the middle of two cabins, the house was called a "saddle-bag," referring to how a saddle-bag laid equally across the back of a horse. A very common house type, one with an open passage between two cabins that shared a long gable roof, was known as a "dog trot." Log construction was good for any building—Sam Houston, "The Raven" to the Cherokees, began his public career teaching in a log cabin schoolhouse outside of Maryville.

But it is one of the great myths of Tennessee that all of its early prominent citizens lived in log houses. Even from 1780 to 1810, that first generation of permanent settlement, some built homes of true architectural distinction. The Carter Mansion in Elizabethton is a testament to building and decorative skills of early Tennessee craftsmen. The intricate masonry and impressive wood paneling of such Georgian-style masterpieces as mighty Cragfont, overlooking Bledsoe's Creek in Sumner County, Hendersonville's Rock Castle, or the Ramsey House in Knoxville, amazes yet today.

Tennesseans early on demonstrated a knack for adapting available building materials to their needs, from yellow poplar logs to what became known as Tennessee marble. The eye for symmetry and balance so characteristic of Georgian style remained dominant in the façades of Tennessee homes for decades. The Cherokees even adapted well to those materials and that directness of Georgian style—as is seen in the reconstructed dwellings at Red Clay in Bradley County, where the Cherokees last gathered before their forced removal to Indian Territory. The president who instigated that removal, Andrew Jackson, also looms large over the legacies of Tennessee architecture. His log "Hermitage" tells how many great plantations started; the second Hermitage, with its impressive two-story Greek Revival portico, reveals the direction of much Tennessee design in the decades before the Civil War.

Classicism is the next dominant theme—be it the four grand porticoes of the Tennessee State Capitol, designed by William Strickland, or the more grafted-on classicism of The Pillars, designed by its owner, John H. Bills in Bolivar. Skilled craftsmen or learned elites were designers of most of Tennessee's great Greek Revival landmarks—the names literally roll off the tongue as a who's who of Tennessee architecture: Belle Meade, Glen Leven, and Belmont in Nashville; Rattle-n-Snap and Hamilton Place in Mount Pleasant; Beersheba Inn in Grundy County; the Rutherford County Courthouse in Murfreesboro; Franklin's Carnton and Harrison House; and Memphis's Hunt-Phelan House.

More than style linked these homes—all were constructed, either wholly or in part—on the backs of African-American slaves. In our own times, as we study and celebrate the landmarks, we also have begun to document the rather different lodgings of the African Americans who were the carpenters, joiners, and masons of these buildings. Antebellum Tennessee is a white-and-black landscape, a reality that is not readily apparent until with astute eyes and open ears we look carefully and listen intently.

The Civil War was a great transformative period in Tennessee history. Often writers assume that Victorian architecture entered Tennessee along with the great changes in citizenship, the economy, and politics brought on by the destruction of the war. However, Tennessee has its antebellum Victorian landmarks. Churches dominated in introducing Gothic style—St. Paul's Episcopal in Franklin, St. Peter Catholic in Memphis, and St. John's Episcopal in Mount Pleasant. But the earliest Gothic was the Hiram Masonic Lodge in Franklin, often overlooked but truly a landmark building in this state. As is Strickland's magnificent Egyptian Revival design of the Downtown Presbyterian Church in Nashville.

Federal occupation forces treated Strickland's church rather poorly, and after the war, the congregation rebuilt, adding a more flamboyant, vigorous Egyptian Revival interior. The changes there mirrored what happened elsewhere. The post-war Victorian styles were livelier, and more driven by the tools and technology of the Industrial Revolution. Rugby in Morgan County introduced a planned village of Carpenter Gothic, Queen Anne, and Arts and Crafts-styled homes, shops, and churches. Adams Street in Memphis was a neighborhood of creative Victorian designs, from the Second Empire-style of the Lee House to the stately eclecticism of the Mallory-Neely House.

Compare the homes to the new multi-story buildings that began to define the skylines of Tennessee's cities. Professional architects were more numerous, and the New South ethos of progress and change built almost new cities. Chattanooga is one significant example—the Dome Building, the Customs House, the MacClellan Building, and the Union Terminal (Chattanooga Choo-Choo) not only documented a city on the rise but also showed what new building materials and technology could achieve. Tennessee began to look more like the rest of the nation, and the great architecture of turn-of-the-century Memphis, for instance, could match anything found in the South.

The New South, unfortunately, also meant the Jim Crow South. African Americans had many of their rights as citizens taken away, or severely limited. For safety and their own visions of prosperity, they developed their own worlds, hidden in their way within the greater landscape of the state. Colleges and churches served as gathering points. Around Fisk University grew Nashville's middle-class African- American neighborhood—a pattern repeated around Knoxville College, Morristown College, Lane College in Jackson, and LeMoyne-Owen College in Memphis.

In rural Tennessee, these African-American enclaves often were forgotten spots on the map—but spots with names that spoke volumes. Promise Land in Dickson County and Free Hills in Clay County are just two examples. By the time of the Great Depression, many of these black communities had newly designed and built schools, typically called Rosenwald schools, for the patron, Julius Rosenwald, who provided the designs, supervision, and some cash. In many Tennessee counties, the local school board also provided funding. But in just as many Tennessee counties, local African Americans not only provided the bulk of the funding, they also provided the labor with which to build their schools. Cairo Rosenwald School in Sumner County, recently restored with help from the Tennessee Preservation Trust and the MTSU Center for Historic Preservation, represents the one-room schoolhouse. The Allen-White School in Hardeman County reveals that some Rosenwald schools were brick, and impressive, as much so as the new public schools constructed for whites from the 1920s into the 1930s.

The lack of ornament and banks of windows characteristic of Rosenwald schools introduced Tennesseans of all races to the functional aesthetic of the modern age. If you missed out on the subtle message that classicism and Victorian styles were out, then a stop at Norris Dam and Village, a massive federal project of the Tennessee Valley Authority and the Civilian Conservation Corps, would clearly introduce the developing brave new world of modern design. A few miles away, during World War II, the message was powerfully reinforced by the stark modernism of Oak Ridge, the "Secret City," and the industrial, commercial, and residential designs of the famous architects William Skidmore and Nathaniel Owings. South of Crossville at Cumberland Homesteads, however, the New Deal showed a more rustic face, one of Crab Orchard stone and understated Tudor Gothic cottages that was more in keeping with the Tennessee vernacular. Rustic style also dominated in our newly established state and national parks, with timber and stone cottages, picnic pavilions, and bath houses creating a modern recreational landscape from Pickett State Park to the Great Smoky Mountains National Park to Meeman-Shelby State Park.

Tennesseans arrived at the new parks in their cars and trucks, and along the drive, they often found a sleek machine aesthetic lining the state's burgeoning roadways. Holiday Inns, one of the most important new firms defining American highways, began in Memphis. We have more than our fair share of classic drive-in restaurants and theaters.

Add to that roadside architecture the Art Deco flourishes found in many of the New Deal's public buildings, from the Federal Courthouse in Chattanooga to the former post office (now the Frist Center for the Arts, in Nashville) and to the Tennessee Office Building (now the John Sevier Building) on Capitol Hill. Tennessee modernism is both reflective of national trends but also grounded in imagery and ideas of the state.

"Grounded in the past, but looking toward new futures"—that is the legacy of the modern historic preservation movement—a determination to prevent sprawl from overtaking decades of growing preservation initiatives. This book has many voices and many stories, but they are all linked to the mission and accomplishments of the Tennessee Preservation Trust. As you enjoy these stories and places, remember it takes the dedication of many to keep them here as legacies for us all. Do your part—join the Tennessee Preservation Trust and make your own stand for Tennessee's treasures.

Carroll Van West, Director
MTSU Center for Historic Preservation

SYCAMORE SHOALS

CARTER COUNTY

— 1775, 1780 —

Sycamore Shoals maintains a double heritage, important not only for land entrepreneur Richard Henderson's purchase from the Cherokees of millions of acres of prime Kentucky and Tennessee real estate, but also for its role as the mustering grounds for the Overmountain Men of Kings Mountain fame.

The region around Sycamore Shoals (present-day Elizabethton) was first settled in the late 1760s by North Carolinians who established the Watauga

Association and formed the first English-speaking independent government west of the Appalachian Mountains. Several years later, on March 17, 1775, Richard Henderson, an associate judge of the North Carolina Superior Court and organizer of the Transylvania Company, met there with a large party of Cherokee Indians. In attendance were several important Cherokee chiefs—Oconostota, the Raven, the Little Carpenter, and Dragging Canoe, among others. Henderson's mission was the American settlement of Central Kentucky and Middle Tennessee, and the purpose of the meeting was to purchase around twenty million acres of real estate from the tribesmen.

Despite strong protests, the treaty was consummated, and the Cherokees received trade goods worth about ten thousand pounds in exchange for the lands strategically located between the Ohio and Cumberland Rivers. Anticipating a successful treaty, Henderson, a few days earlier, had dispatched Daniel Boone and an exploring

Colonel John Sevier was a commander of the "Overmountain Men," and would later serve as governor of the short-lived State of Franklin, and then as the first governor for the State of Tennessee.

3

Lloyd Branson painting depicting the mustering of the Overmountain Men, courtesy of the Tennessee State Museum

party, to clear a path through the wilderness from the Long Island of the Holston (present-day Kingsport) to Central Kentucky. Henderson followed Boone the following week.

Success in Kentucky was not to be in Henderson's future. Soon after the treaty signing, Virginia's royal governor, Lord Dunmore, issued a proclamation disclaiming the Kentucky purchase, and, in July, 1777, the Virginia House of Delegates voided the entire deal. With his dreams of a Kentucky empire now dashed, Henderson turned his attention toward his smaller Tennessee holdings, determined to establish a permanent settlement at the Great French Lick on the Cumberland River (Nashville).

Five and one-half years after Henderson's treaty with the Cherokees, Sycamore Shoals achieved a second claim to fame. During the Revolutionary War, on September 25, 1780, more than one thousand Virginians, North Carolinians, and soon-to-be Tennesseans gathered for a military expedition to counter recent inroads in the Carolinas by British Major Patrick Ferguson and his American loyalist army. Samuel Doak, the renowned churchman who is often referred to as the "father" of education in Tennessee, delivered his famous "Sword of the Lord and Gideon" sermon to the militiamen as they organized their units under the joint command of Colonels Isaac Shelby, John Sevier, and William Campbell.

Leaving Sycamore Shoals the following day, the army marched south, crossing the Appalachian Mountains and arriving at Quaker Meadows near present-day Morganton, North Carolina, on September 30, where they were joined by around 350 additional North Carolinians, anxious for battle. The enlarged army continued southward and three days later arrived at Gilbert Town, expecting to find Major Ferguson and his loyalist army, but to no avail. Picking up more volunteers along the way, the army, now swollen to around 1,800 men, reached Kings Mountain, located just south of the North Carolina-South Carolina border, on October 7.

Ferguson's threats to "march his army over the mountains, hang their leaders and lay their country waste with fire and sword" were still ringing in the ears of the Overmountain Men as they immediately engaged the loyalist forces. In the confusion of battle, Ferguson allowed the *crème de la crème* of his loyalist army to be surrounded by the patriot forces, and when the sixty-five-minute encounter

Two of the four iron kettles used by Mary Patton to manufacture the 500 pounds of gunpowder used by the Overmountain Men during the campaign into South Carolina

"Go forth...to the aid of your brethren, the defense of your liberty and the protection of your homes. And may the God of Justice be with you and you victory."

Samuel Doak

was over, the British major had lost nearly nine hundred men either killed, wounded, or captured. Ferguson was hit multiple times by patriot rifle fire as he rode back and forth attempting to marshal his soldiers. He soon died of his wounds and was buried on the battlefield. The Overmountain Men lost around ninety men killed and wounded.

The Battle of Kings Mountain was the decisive turning point of the Revolutionary War in the South, setting the stage for the American army's victory at Yorktown. Thousands of Americans who had maintained their loyalty to the Crown stood aghast at the total routing of Ferguson's army. The British commander, Lord Charles Cornwallis, was forced back into South Carolina and his intended invasion of North Carolina had to be delayed for a year. The tide had finally turned against the British army and victory would soon come to the infant United States.

"Sweet Lips," the gun that turned the tide for America in the Revolution, fired the shot that mortally wounded the ruthless British Major Patrick Ferguson at the Battle of Kings Mountain, South Carolina.

Sycamore Shoals and the adjacent land are administered by Tennessee State Parks as the Sycamore Shoals State Historic Area.

CARTER MANSION

⟶ pre-1780 ⟵

The Carter Mansion, the first frame house constructed in Tennessee, is possibly the only remaining link to the Watauga Association, and one of the oldest houses remaining in the state.

John Carter and his son, Landon, built the home known locally as "the Mansion" some time prior to 1780 on part of a huge land acquisition located in present-day upper East Tennessee. The Carters migrated from Virginia and were among the early Watauga pioneers living in the Carter's Valley settlement. In 1772, John was elected chairman of the court for the Watauga Association. Upon John's death in 1781, Landon inherited his father's huge estate. Meanwhile, he served as secretary of state for the State of Franklin from 1784–89. When Tennessee entered the Union in 1796, the General Assembly created Carter County, named in Landon's honor. The seat of government for the new county was named Elizabethton, in honor of Landon's wife, Elizabeth.

One of the most charming features of the three-room mansion, reputed to be the oldest frame house in Tennessee, is the beautiful wood paneling that graces the walls of the entrance hall and other rooms. The hall, described by one historian as possessing "all the dignity of a hall in one of the eighteenth century Virginia houses along the James," contains a large fireplace. Its two overmantel landscape paintings are among the most important works of frontier-era art in Tennessee.

Other members of this illustrious Tennessee family were Landon Carter's son, William Blount Carter, and his grandson, Samuel Powhatan Carter. William was a veteran of the War of 1812 and later served in both the Tennessee House of Representatives and Senate, as well as in the United States House of Representatives. Samuel is believed to be the only man in American history to have attained the ranks of both general in the army and admiral in the navy.

The folk scenes painted directly onto the walls over the mantels were probably the work of a traveling artist and likely depicted scenes from Carter's native Tidewater Virginia and ancestral Scotland.

Carter Mansion is administered as part of the Sycamore Shoals State Historic Area by Tennessee State Parks.

ROCKY MOUNT

SULLIVAN COUNTY

→ *original house 1772* ←

Rocky Mount served as the first capital of Tennessee's predecessor, the Territory of the United States South of the River Ohio.

During late October 1790, William Blount, the newly appointed governor of the Territory of the United States South of the River Ohio, rode up to the log home of William Cobb, in present-day Sullivan County. In his journal, Blount wrote, "On the 11th instant, I arrived in this country.... I am very well accommodated with a Room with Glass Windows, Fireplace, Etc., at this place." The aristocratic Blount had no doubt experienced more lavish amenities during his travels, but, here on the remote western frontier, Cobb's cozy home was much appreciated.

Blount had departed Washington, North Carolina, the previous August to assume his new position across the mountains as governor, soon establishing temporary territorial headquarters at Cobb's residence, Rocky Mount. From that point forward, much of the official correspondence of Governor Blount and Secretary Daniel Smith was prefaced with either "Territory of the United States of America South of the River Ohio. At William Cobbs" or "Mr. Cobb's near Jonesborough." Rocky Mount was replaced as the capital when the seat of government moved to Knoxville in 1792.

Treaty of Holston signed with the Cherokees by William Blount while serving at Rocky Mount as governor of the Southwest Territory.

The first dwelling on this site was originally built by Cobb, one of the earliest and most influential residents in the Watauga Settlements, soon after his arrival in the region around 1770. The present house dates to the late 1820s. Andrew Jackson once boarded with the Cobb family while awaiting his law license.

Rocky Mount is owned by the State of Tennessee and administered by the Tennessee Historical Commission through the Rocky Mount Historical Association.

9

TIPTON-HAYNES SITE
WASHINGTON COUNTY
—◆ c. 1783 ◆—

Dreams of Franklin becoming the nation's fourteenth state died in February 1788, when John Sevier and his followers were routed at John Tipton's homeplace in Johnson City.

Between 1784 and 1788, while hoards of land-hungry Americans were pouring into the Ohio River Valley and the Northwest Territory, residents of a large portion of present-day East Tennessee organized a political entity, which, had it been successful, would have resulted in it, not Vermont, being the country's fourteenth state. It was called Franklin, and it came about as a result of the concern shared by settlers in the region over their sudden loss of governmental oversight and security caused by North Carolina's relinquishment of its far western expanses (present-day Tennessee) to the federal establishment. In 1784, John Sevier was named first and only chief executive and the capital was established at Jonesborough. Congress never recognized Franklin, and its territory reverted to North Carolina in 1788.

The present-day counties eventually encompassed by the proposed state of Franklin included: Johnson, Carter, Sullivan, Washington, Unicoi, Hawkins, Greene, Cocke, Jefferson, Hamblen, Sevier, and Blount. Initial supporters of the movement for statehood included John Sevier, Colonel Arthur Campbell, William Cocke, and the Reverend Samuel Houston, the father of Sam Houston of Texas fame. Among the eventual opponents were John Tipton and two governors of North Carolina, Alexander Martin and Richard Caswell.

In his manifesto of April 25, 1785, denouncing the newly formed state,

Portrait of Landon Carter Haynes painted by Samuel Shaver in the mid-1850s

John Tipton's early cabin on the Tipton-Haynes farm site

Governor Martin declared, "Designs of a more dangerous nature and deeper die seem to glare in the western revolt.... I have thought proper to issue this manifesto, hereby warning all persons concerned in the said revolt...that the honour of this State {North Carolina} has been particularly wounded."

Continuing, he pleaded with the Franklinites to "let your proposals be consistent with the honour of the State {and} by your allegiance as good citizens...I make no doubt but her generosity, in time, will meet your wishes."

The verbal bantering between the two factions solved none of the thorny problems that existed between those who wanted Franklin to become the nation's fourteenth state, and those who simply wanted the vast piece of real estate returned to the control of North Carolina. The people who mattered most to the Franklinites were the members of the Continental Congress, who had to approve the entry of the new state into the Union. Approval from two-thirds of the existing thirteen states, or nine votes, was required for passage of the enabling act, but when the role was called in the spring of 1785, the

Harper's Magazine 1857 illustration of the Tipton-Haynes Farm

measure garnered only seven votes. The issue reached international proportions in London, when the stately and politically connected *Gentleman's Magazine* sympathized with the Franklinites, reporting in an August 1785 issue that "the people of the western counties found themselves grievously taxed without enjoying the blessings of it."

The ticklish issue climaxed during February 1788, when John Sevier and a group of supporters laid siege to John Tipton's farmhouse near Johnson City. The home, measuring 25 feet by 35 feet was built of logs as a defense against Indian attack. Tipton, a former recruiting officer during the Revolution and presently a North Carolina official, had earlier detained several of Sevier's slaves for his non-payment of state taxes, causing such anger in Sevier that he assembled a sizeable group of supporters and marched on Tipton. With Tipton were about forty of his associates. The confrontation, sometimes referred to as the Battle of the Lost State of Franklin, lasted for the better part of two days, with minimal casualties on either side. The siege was lifted when reinforcements appeared and routed Sevier and his command. For all intent and purposes, the brief life of the State of Franklin was over.

In the mid-1850s, Haynes constructed his law office, in the Greek Revival style, next to his home.

The life of John Sevier was spared, allowing him to pursue greater opportunities, not the least of which was his election in 1796 as Tennessee's first governor. As for Tipton, he assisted in the drafting of the Tennessee constitution and went on to serve in both the state House of Representatives and the Senate. Tipton's house eventually passed to his son, John Tipton, Jr., who, like his father, served in the General Assembly. In 1839, Landon Carter Haynes, an attorney, future state legislator, and future member of the Confederate States of America senate, was presented the Tipton Farm as a wedding present.

Today, the Tipton-Haynes State Historic Site consists of the elder Tipton's original log cabin, his two-story frame, "glorified pioneer" home, and several other dependencies, the most prominent of which is Landon Carter Haynes's Greek Revival-styled frame law office.

Tipton-Haynes Farm is owned by the State of Tennessee and administered by the Tennessee Historical Commission through the Tipton-Haynes Historical Association.

MAIN STREET
JONESBOROUGH
WASHINGTON COUNTY

⁘ 1779 ⁘

Even before Jonesborough entered the pages of recorded history,
the region thereabout was a fabled land, sacred to the Cherokee
Indians, one of America's most significant tribes.

Jonesborough is the oldest organized town in Tennessee, dating from 1779
when the North Carolina legislature named the village to become the seat of
government for Washington County (North Carolina), which had been established

14

two years earlier as the first county in present-day Tennessee. The town was
named in honor of Willie (pronounced Wiley) Jones, an influential North
Carolinian who was a strong advocate for his native state's westward expansion.

Seven different courthouses have served the county—the first, a small log
structure built by James Carter around 1778, and the last, the present-day
building, designed by the architectural firm of Baumann and Baumann in
1912–13. The clock, facing in all four directions, taken from the 1847 courthouse,
was placed in the existing structure and continues to give time.

Jonesborough is noted for several historical events that occurred in the region
throughout the years. Almost a decade before the first white settlers established the
nearby Watauga Settlements, the noted frontiersman Daniel Boone hunted the
dense forests. Upon a giant beech tree located between present-day Jonesborough
and Blountville, he carved his famous message, "D. Boon CILLED A BAR on Tree
in THE YEAR 1760." In 1784, Jonesborough became the capital of the ill-fated
"Lost State of Franklin," an abortive attempt of residents of the western section of

Porch of the Chester
Inn and the
Washington County
Courthouse

North Carolina (present-day East Tennessee) to form their own state government
and be admitted to the Union as the fourteenth state. It provided an early
Tennessee home to Andrew Jackson, who lived for a brief time in an early 1770s,
two-story, clapboard cabin owned by Major Christopher Taylor, and was admitted
to the bar while a resident. Shortly after the Tennessee Constitution authorized the
creation of a state seal in 1796, Jonesborough silversmiths Matthew and William
Atkinson were commissioned to design and engrave the device. However, the state
legislature failed to approve a measure allowing the seal, delaying its use until the
administration of Tennessee's second governor, Archibald Roane.

In 1797, William P. Chester, a Pennsylvania physician, built an inn and
hostelry on Main Street and his accommodations satisfied all three Tennessee
presidents—Andrew Jackson, James K. Polk, and neighbor Andrew Johnson—as
well as the state's first governor, John Sevier.

Jonesborough
Presbyterian Church,
built during the 1840s

During 1819, Jacob Howard published a small newspaper titled the *Manumission Intelligencer*. Financed and edited by devout abolitionist Elihu Embree, the paper enjoyed an initial success and was soon replaced by another periodical

called the *Emancipator*, also issued by Howard and Embree. The two newspapers were the nation's first periodicals devoted to abolition issues. By the time Embree died in October 1820, circulation had grown to nearly two thousand readers, and issues of the *Emancipator* had been distributed to practically every state governor in the South.

Two obscure names in Tennessee history have strong connections with Jonesborough. Virginia-born Thomas Kemmerson (1773–1837), the first mayor of Knoxville and a judge on the Tennessee Superior Court and State Supreme Court, lived near town and for a

Chester Inn, built in the late 1790s, is the oldest frame structure in Jonesborough, and accommodated Presidents Andrew Jackson, James K. Polk, and Andrew Johnson.

Preservation of the Christopher Taylor House was a keystone of the town's restoration effort. A young Andrew Jackson boarded here while living briefly in Jonesborough.

while was the editor of the *Washington Republican and Farmer's Journal*. Alfred Eugene Jackson (1807–1889), native-born businessman, was an executive with the East Tennessee & Virginia Railroad and later served as a brigadier general in the Confederate army, distinguishing himself at the Battle of Saltville in 1864.

"This is the place where the celebrated convention for forming the government of Frankland [Franklin] sat in 1784.... [A] convention of deputies from the counties of Washington, Sullivan, and Green [sic], assembled at Jonesboro' [and] appointed John Sevier, President, and Landon Clark, Clerk.... and the new State was named Frankland."

Eastin Morris, in *The Tennessee Gazetteer*, 1834

Spring in Jonesborough

1930 Fourth of July
parade celebrating
Jonesborough's
sesquicentennial

Young citizen riding
cow and leading
herd past Chester
Inn in 1915

1890 Masonic parade

1914 funeral procession of
Henry Jackson, County Trustee

Through the late-twentieth-century preservation efforts of the Heritage Alliance, Main Street Jonesborough endures as the heart
of one of America's favorite small towns.

DAVY CROCKETT BIRTHPLACE

— Crockett born in 1786 —

"…the most singular, and in many respects the most remarkable, man in the history of the pioneer settlement in the great west was without a moment's consideration of others…Davy Crockett."

William F. "Buffalo Bill" Cody, 1888

"Born on a mountaintop in Tennessee, greenest state in the land of the free." So goes the 1950s ode to one of America's most enduring heroes, David Crockett. The song's popularity and the phenomenal rise in Crockett's reputation occurred when Hollywood spun its magic with the frontier icon. However, the mid-twentieth century was not the first time that Crockett's name was on everyone's lips. His colorful and backwoods reputation in the halls of the U. S. Congress, punctuated by his glaring opposition to President Andrew Jackson's Indian policies—and assisted in no small measure by a series of spurious, ghost-written "almanacs" published during his own lifetime—made him a living legend.

Crockett was born on August 17, 1786, in a small log cabin near the confluence of the Nolichucky River and Big Limestone Creek in present-day Greene County, Tennessee, the son of John and Rebecca Hawkins Crockett. The property encompassing his birthplace was owned by land speculator George Gillespie and was already steeped in history, being part of Jacob Brown's Nolichucky settlements, which, along with the Watauga Association, represented the first organized communities in Tennessee. The region was still heavily visited by Indians—in fact, young David's own grandparents had only recently been killed by tribesmen several miles away. The present-day cabin is reconstructed, but is

Cover of one in a series of Davy Crockett almanacs extolling the tall tales and heroic deeds of Crockett, which were immensely popular in the mid-nineteenth century and contributed to his continuing national legend.

consistent with the size and appearance of the original structure.

The lush, hardwood forest that surrounded Crockett's birthplace provided much joy and entertainment for the youngster. There, he developed many of the outdoor skills that he would call upon later during his years as an Indian fighter, frontier farmer, and defender of the Alamo. Situated on the western slopes of the lengthy Appalachian Mountain chain that ran from Maine to Georgia, the territory was among the first settled in the South by Anglos following the French and Indian War and was in direct violation of King George III's *Proclamation of 1763*, which banned white settlement west of the mountains' crest. But the proximity of various Indian tribes, primarily the Cherokee, also gave Crockett an insight into the blissful way of life that these natives shared with nature and with each other. No doubt, Crockett's early years near his birthplace also assisted in the development of strong political ideals that would follow him during the remainder of his life.

From his birthplace in the eastern part of the state, he eventually moved to present-day Middle Tennessee—to Lawrence, Moore, and Franklin Counties—and was elected to the General Assembly during this period. Later, he moved to Gibson County in West Tennessee, whence he served in the U. S. House of Representatives from 1827–1831 and again from 1833–1835. In 1835, when he lost his bid for reelection to Andrew Jackson supporter, Adam Huntsman, he is reported to have declared to his former constituency, that they "could go to hell and I'll go to Texas."

On November 1, 1835, Crockett—who, according to his daughter, was "dressed in his hunting suit, wearing a coon skin cap"— left home, family, and friends in Rutherford, Tennessee. During early February 1836, with a cadre of volunteers, he rode into the old Spanish mission called the Alamo, in San Antonio, Texas, determined to keep it free from the Mexican army, led by General Antonio López de Santa Anna, who had vowed to overrun the structure and return the newly declared Republic of Texas to the Mexican people.

In late February 1836, Santa Anna's troops besieged the Alamo and on the morning of March 6, they launched their final assault. Within less than an hour, absolute silence prevailed and the gallant men of the Alamo, including David Crockett, lay dead.

Opposite page:
A Crockett family history as recorded on the pages of the family Bible

Davy Crockett's powder horn

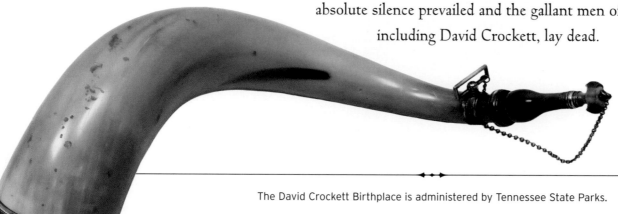

The David Crockett Birthplace is administered by Tennessee State Parks.

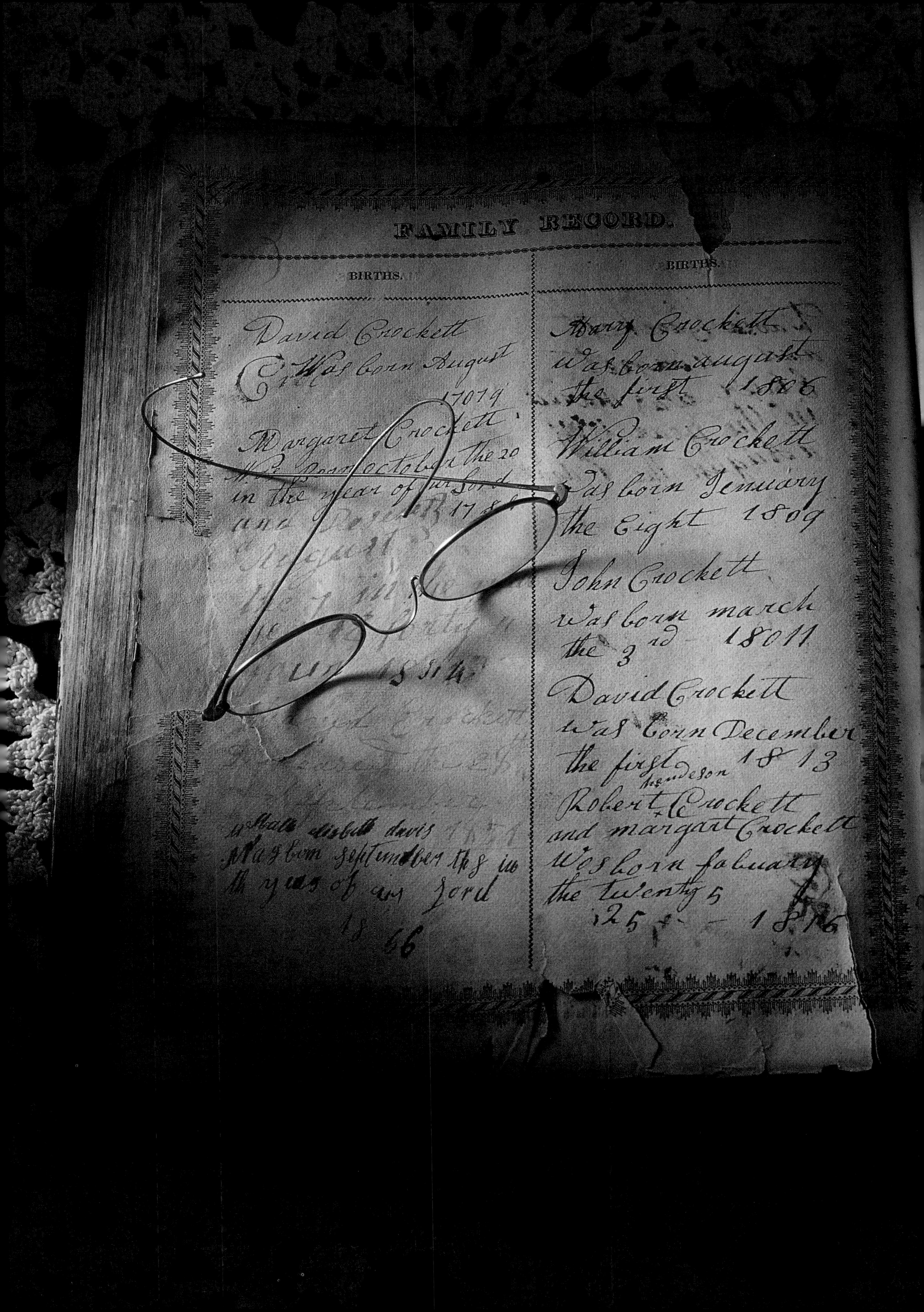

FAMILY RECORD.

BIRTHS.	BIRTHS.

David Crockett
was born August
1079

Margaret Crockett
was born October the 20
in the year of our Lord
one thousand 178

Mary Crockett
was born august
the first 1806

William Crockett
was born January
the Eight 1809

John Crockett
was born march
the 3rd 18011

David Crockett
was born December
the first henderson 1813

Robert Crockett
and margart Crockett
was born fabuary
the twenty 5
25 1816

Matilda elisbith davis
was born september th 8 in
th year of our Lord
1866

PRESIDENT ANDREW JOHNSON HOME

GREENE COUNTY

first house c. 1830s
second house c. 1851

America's presidents have hailed from all walks of life, including farming, public service, the military, journalism, and the legal profession, among others. Few, however, have had more practical experience than Andrew Johnson in serving in such a variety of legislative and executive offices at every level of government: local, state, and federal. During his long career, he filled the positions of city alderman, city mayor, state representative, state senator, U.S. representative, governor, U.S. senator, vice president, and president of the United States.

Matthew Brady portrait of Andrew Johnson as vice president

Opposite: Andrew Johnson's early Greeneville home across from the tailor's shop, owned prior to becoming vice president

Thirty-eight and a half years passed from the time Andrew Johnson (1808–1875), a North Carolina tailor, arrived almost penniless in Greeneville in 1826 until he became the seventeenth president of the United States upon Abraham Lincoln's death in 1865. The years between the two dates were filled with activity more aligned with politics than with the tailor's pursuit of private enterprise. Three years after settling in the town, Johnson was elected an alderman, thus beginning a long career of public service.

By the 1830s, Johnson and his wife, Eliza McCardell Johnson (1810–1876), and family were living in a modest, two-story brick house on the corner of College and Depot Streets. Nearby was his frame tailor shop, purchased at a sheriff's sale around 1830 and moved to the site. The Johnsons

Early view of the Johnson tailors shop with the early home visible in the background

Johnson's tailor's shears

occupied this home until 1851 when they moved to a larger structure located a couple of blocks away on Main Street. Called the Homestead, the imposing house was two stories, with a one-story ell. A second story was added to the ell in 1868–69, when Johnson planned his return to Greeneville from Washington, D.C. The façade displays strong Federal design characteristics, and several Greek Revival features are present as well, including the columned doorway with side lights, the transom, and the brick cornices with dentils.

In the meantime, Johnson had become financially stable and owned a 350-acre farm outside of town and several flour mills and town lots. "There is no use in buying property unless there is a bargain in it," he once told his son. By the time of the family's move to the Homestead, Johnson had abandoned his tailoring business and was involved in full-time politics. His election as city alderman of Greeneville in 1829 fired his intense interest in governmental affairs which continued to grow until he successfully attained the offices of mayor of Greeneville, state representative, state senator, and U.S. congressman. In 1853, two years following the relocation to the larger home, the family moved to Nashville to be with Johnson, who had been elected governor that year. He was the first governor to be inaugurated in the new Tennessee State Capitol.

"Let peace and prosperity be restored to the land.
May God bless this people: may God save the Constitution."

Andrew Johnson in the U.S. Senate, March 22, 1875

Following his two terms as governor, Johnson was elected to the U.S. Senate, where he served until he was appointed military governor of Tennessee in 1862 after the outbreak of the Civil War. In the 1864 elections, he successfully ran as President Abraham Lincoln's vice-presidential running mate and became president upon Lincoln's death by assassination in April 1865. During his term in office, he oversaw the purchase of Alaska, received the first queen ever to visit the White

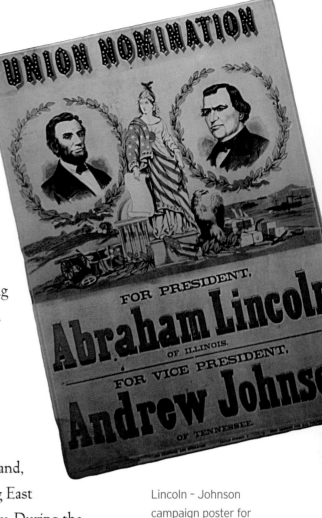

House, vetoed the controversial Tenure of Office Act and the Military Reconstruction Bill, and was impeached by the House of Representatives but acquitted by the Senate by one vote. Returning to Greeneville, he ran for the U.S. Senate twice, and was defeated twice, but in 1875 took his old Senate seat, becoming the only president ever to serve in the Senate after the presidency.

Andrew Johnson died in Carter County, Tennessee, in 1875 and is buried in the Andrew Johnson National Cemetery in Greeneville, along with his wife who died six months later.

As an American president, Andrew Johnson has been much maligned—generally in the American South and specifically in Tennessee—as a Northern sympathizer who "sold out" his homeland, and who cast his future with Northern interests. As a slave-owning East Tennessean, a position rare at the time, the man is truly an anomaly. During the Civil War, as vice president, he defended the Federal government's authority to militarily enforce Southern subservience to President Abraham Lincoln's edict of sustaining the Union at any price, yet, shortly after war's end, as president, he demanded that Reconstruction be a short-lived "evil" that would, as soon as possible, once again place Southern states on an equal footing with those in the North.

Lincoln - Johnson campaign poster for the 1864 election

Johnson's tomb in the Andrew Johnson National Cemetery in Greeneville, looking out to the Unaka Mountains

Following spread: Andrew Johnson's Main Street "Homeplace" residence following the years of presidency

Andrew Johnson's gravesite, the Homestead, and his earlier 1830 home are part of the Andrew Johnson National Historic Site, which is administered by the U.S. National Park Service.

ROGERSVILLE

⸺ *early 1780s* ⸺

Rogersville was the site of the first newspaper ever printed in present-day Tennessee, the Knoxville Gazette, so named in anticipation of the upcoming move of the territorial capital to Knoxville. Answering the invitation of Southwest Territory Governor William Blount, the paper was established on November 5, 1791, by George Roulstone and Robert Ferguson, lately of North Carolina.

When Irish-born Joseph Rogers settled in present-day Hawkins County during the early 1780s, probably the last thing on his mind was that he would fall in love with the daughter of a wealthy Revolutionary War land grant recipient in the area and eventually become the founder of the town of Rogersville. The region was only beginning to be frequented by pioneer families and merchants, eager to leave their homes east of the Appalachians and start life anew. Among the first migrants to this wilderness region were David Crockett's grandparents, who were killed in 1778 by Indians and are buried in present-day Rogers Cemetery. Just a few years after his arrival and marriage to Mary Amis, Rogers built a hostelry called Rogers' Tavern located in town along the Great Valley Road connecting the Pennsylvania settlements with those in the southern trans-Appalachian region.

Rogers maintained more or less a monopoly on travelers' business until 1825, when John A. McKinney, an attorney and judge, built a more elaborate establishment, today's Hale Springs Inn. The three-story, Federal brick building rented its several

Joseph Rogers Building c. 1810, served the town's founder variously as a store, post office, bank, office, and private residence.

Rosemont, c. 1842 –
built by John A.
McKinney as a
wedding gift to his
daughter

guest rooms to weary travelers and provided tasty fare as well. All three of
Tennessee's presidents—Andrew Jackson, James K. Polk, and Andrew Johnson—
have been guests at the Inn. The first of the three, Jackson, still in office at the
time, is said to have chosen Hale Springs Inn to spend the night over the nearby
Rogers' Tavern because the Inn had a balcony over the front door from which he
could make a speech to the townspeople. In 1998, when the Inn closed for
business, it was noted as the longest-operating hotel in Tennessee.

The Hawkins County Courthouse was built in 1836 and is one of only six
in Tennessee dating prior to the Civil War. It is the state's second oldest such
structure, antedated only by the Dickson County Courthouse in Charlotte,
erected in 1833. John Damron of neighboring Sullivan County designed the

*"In 1833, it [Rogersville] contained about three hundred inhabitants, four
lawyers, two doctors, two divines, one academy, seven stores, three taverns, six
blacksmiths, three bricklayers, four carpenters, four cabinet makers, two painters,
two hatters, four tailors, four shoemakers, two saddlers, one silversmith, three
tanners, one tinner, and four wagonmakers."*

Eastin Morris, in *The Tennessee Gazetteer*, 1834

Built in 1845 as the Bank of the State of Tennessee, this building is home to Tennessee's oldest Masonic lodge in continuous operation - Overton Lodge #4 F. & A. M., chartered 1805.

building, which has been renovated twice since, in 1870 and 1929, at which time the church-like steeple was added. Its four columns are built of bricks, and a unique door is present in the front wall on the second-story level. During the Civil War, the structure was occupied at various times by both Confederate and Union troops.

Rogersville's founder, Joseph Rogers, as well as the grandparents of Davy Crockett who were killed by Indians in 1777, are buried in the Rogers Cemetery.

East Main Street, Mitchell's Tavern, c. 1815 - At this site, in 1791, printer George Roulston began publishing the *Knoxville Gazette*, first newspaper printed in the Territory South of the River Ohio. During the 1820's the former newspaper office was Mitchell's Tavern before being razed in 1830 and the present building constructed as a grocery and hardware store.

Rogersville's Masonic Hall houses the oldest continuously operating Masonic lodge in Tennessee. Named in honor of John Overton, Andrew Jackson's law partner and owner of Nashville's Traveller's Rest, the Overton Lodge #5 Free and Accepted Masons was chartered in 1805. The building in which the lodge meets was completed in 1839 and first occupied by a branch of the Bank of Tennessee. Following the Civil War, the bank failed and the structure passed through several owners before being acquired by Lodge #5.

Rogersville is among Tennessee's oldest towns and boasts an eminent history. Confederate Lieutenant General Alexander Peter "A.P." Stewart was born there in 1821. One of the C.S.A.'s most outstanding commanders, he graduated from the U.S. Military Academy in 1842. Resigning from the army, he later taught at West Point, Cumberland University in Lebanon, and the University of Nashville. He opposed secession, but joined the Confederate army in 1861 as a major of artillery, eventually commanding brigades at Shiloh, Murfreesboro, Chickamauga, and Atlanta. Following the war, he returned to a professorship at Cumberland University and afterward served as chancellor of the University of Mississippi. He died in 1908.

Rogersville is also noted for its educational history. Early on in the town's existence, McMinn Academy, a successful military school, was built there, and in 1849, the Rogersville Synodical College, a Presbyterian-operated finishing school for women, enrolled girls and young ladies from throughout the region. From 1883 until 1955, Swift College for African Americans, also run by the Presbyterian Church, attained a stellar reputation.

On the site of this 1830 building, George Roulston printed the *Knoxville Gazette*, the first newspaper published in the Territory South of the River Ohio.

Built in 1836, the Hawkins County Courthouse is the oldest original courthouse still in use in Tennessee.

Classic Palladian window, Hawkins County Courthouse

Next spread: Hale Springs Inn, built in 1824, was a favorite stop for President Jackson traveling by stagecoach between Nashville and Washington.

Hale Springs Inn operates as a newly renovated, refurbished bed-and-breakfast inn, operated by the Rogersville Heritage Association.

BLOUNT MANSION

KNOX COUNTY

—◄► 1792 ►◄—

One of Tennessee's eminent historians, John Trotwood Moore, once termed the Blount Mansion as "the most important historical spot in Tennessee." And why should this not be so? Designated the capital of the State of Tennessee's predecessor, the Territory of the United States South of the River Ohio, the site represents the genesis of everything historical that has transpired in Tennessee since the territory's formation in 1790.

William Blount (1749–1800) was born in North Carolina and as a young man participated in the Battle of Alamance in 1771, a conflict which pitted North Carolina patriots (of which Blount was one) and the forces of the British royal governor, William Tryon. Later, he held seats in the North Carolina General Assembly, the Continental Congress, and the Constitutional Convention of 1787. Failing in his attempts to be elected North Carolina's first U.S. senator, Blount turned his eyes westward across the Appalachians, where he controlled a considerable amount of land.

In late December 1789, the North Carolina General Assembly relinquished its western holdings (from the crest of the Appalachian Mountains to the Mississippi River) to the United States government with the intention that these lands be organized with territorial status. Federal authorities accepted the cession and, in early April 1790, so advised North Carolina officials.

The following month, the Territory of the United States South of the River Ohio was organized, following the precedent for the earlier formation of the Northwest Territory. At the suggestion of Dr. Hugh Williamson, Timothy Bloodworth, and John B. Ashe—all congressmen

Portrait of William Blount painted around 1845 by Washington B. Cooper from a life miniature of Blount

Engraving of Blount
Mansion visitor, Louis
Philippe, who was
later to become king
of France

from North Carolina—President George Washington
appointed William Blount as the territorial governor, Daniel
Smith as secretary, and David Campbell, William Peery, and
John McNairy as judges. In response to his appointment, Blount
wrote Secretary of State Thomas Jefferson, saying that "I accept it
[the commission] with a firm Determination to perform the duties of it
to the best of [my] Abilities."

In late August, Blount departed Washington, North Carolina, to pursue his
territorial responsibilities across the mountains. By early 1791, he had established
temporary territorial headquarters at William Cobb's residence, Rocky Mount, in
present-day Sullivan County. During 1792, Blount moved the territorial capital
southwest to Knoxville and administered governmental affairs from his home, built
the same year. Throughout the remainder of the territorial period and until the
State of Tennessee's organization occurred in 1796, the Blount Mansion held its
position as the seat of government.

*"I have determined to make the Place where the Treaty was held
the place of my future Residence and shall honor it with the name of Knox-Ville it
is on the North Bank of the Holston about four Miles below the Mouth of the
French Broad…from Chota forty miles…."*

William Blount, 1791

Governor Blount's imposing home was one of the earliest frame houses built
west of the Appalachians and the first in the region to have glass windows, prompting
curious visiting Cherokees to call it the "house with a hundred eyes." Situated along
the Holston River, Blount Mansion consisted of two-and-one-half stories and was the
first dwelling, other than log structures, in the fledgling village that was to become
Knoxville. It contained spacious, well-appointed rooms, with floors and walls made
from pine heartwood. The formal gardens extended to the river, a distance of around
150 feet, and contained a large variety of shrubs, flowers, fruit trees, vegetables, herbs,
and ornamental plants, all arranged along a series of terraces that sloped from the
house to the river. The site selected for the home was close by the spot where Blount
and representatives of the Cherokee Indians signed the landmark Treaty of the

Holston the previous year.

Celebrated visitors to Blount's home included young Andrew Jackson and Louis Philippe, a refugee from the French Revolution and future king of France. The nobleman recorded in the journal of his travels the experience of bathing in the Holston River and, years later, recounted in the royal court the strange practice of "Tennesseans sleeping three-to-a-bed."

Blount's administration was fraught with many challenges, not the least of which was the attempted cessation of bloodshed between white settlers living in the Mero District and dissident Cherokee Indians of the Lower Towns along the Tennessee River (called Chickamaugas) and their Creek and Shawnee allies. Federal officials, led by President George Washington himself, were adamant that Mero residents refrain from pursuing offensive warfare against the natives, despite the almost continual skirmishing between the two factions. Finally, in late 1794, when General James Robertson of Nashville—against orders—dispatched several hundred militia on a successful mission to destroy the Chickamauga towns of Nickajack and Running Water, peace on the far frontier was restored.

In January 1796, Governor Blount hosted a convention at Blount Mansion with the purpose of framing a constitution for the forthcoming State of Tennessee. With himself as president of the convention, delegates ordained that the State's first legislative session would be held in late March, at which time General John Sevier was elected governor and William Blount tendered his resignation, confident that "I have left the Frontiers in a perfect State of Peace." The federal act admitting Tennessee as the sixteenth state to the Union was approved by both houses of Congress on June 1, 1796, and the Territory of the United States South of the River Ohio was no more.

Blount's territorial capital office, a few short garden steps from the home

William and Mary Blount are buried in the First Presbyterian Cemetery, the first burial ground in Knoxville.

Blount Mansion is administered by the Blount Mansion Association.

RAMSEY HOUSE

⟶ 1797 ⟵

With its strength and massive stone construction, the Ramsey House is in the same league with Middle Tennessee's Cragfont and Rock Castle.

When Colonel Francis A. Ramsey (1764–1820) and his family arrived near the infant town of Knoxville, the village had only recently been designated the capital of the new state of Tennessee. Ramsey, one of the first settlers in the area, had already served as an official in Washington County government and participated in the organization of both the State of Franklin and the Southwest Territory. A committed public servant, he eventually devoted thirty-seven years of his life to government activity.

Ramsey settled about ten miles out of town in an area called Swan Pond, named for a small lake that teemed with swans, geese, ducks, and other waterfowl. He hired Knoxville architect Thomas Hope, an Englishman who had migrated to Charleston, South Carolina, forty years earlier, to draw the plans. The design that Hope created for Ramsey was a simple, two-story, stone house made with locally quarried red marble and trimmed with blue limestone. The house is rectangular in shape, measuring about forty-by-twenty-five feet, with an ell, probably used as a kitchen, extending from one side. Chimneys flank each end of the main structure and another one serves the ell and contains an outside oven. The hallway, dominated by a staircase to the second floor and its three rooms, runs the entire depth of the house, with large parlors on either side.

One of Colonel Ramsey's sons was the eminent historian J. G. M. (James Gettys McGready) Ramsey (1797–1884), born the year the Ramsey House was completed. The younger Ramsey graduated from Washington College (Tennessee) in 1816,

Sampler stitched in 1811 by Col. Ramsey's daughter, Eliza Jane Naomi Ramsey, to commemorate the earlier deaths of her mother and four brothers

Oh Death! thou canker-worm of human joy!
Thou cruel foe to sweet domestick peace!
He soon shall come who shall thy shafts destroy
And cause thy dreadfull ravages to cease.
  Yes the Redemer comes to wipe the tears
The briny tears from every weeping eye
And Death and sin and doubts and gloomy fears
Shall all be lost in endless victory.

William Baine Alexander Ramsey Died March the 21st 1799, wanting 8 days of 8 years of age.
Samuel Reynolds Ramsey Died September the 16th 1800. aged 5 years and 38 days.
Francis Alexander Ramsey Died November the 23d 1804 Aged five weeks and one day.

Peggy A. Ramsey Mother of the above named Children died July 7th 1805. Aged 39 years three months and four days.
John McKnitt Alexander Ramsey Died March the 27th 1808. Aged 14 years 10 months and 28 days.

Detail of the pink rough cut marble and blue limestone corner quoins and window lintels. The carved cornice modillions are a result of architect Thomas Hope's Charleston background and are extremely decorative for a frontier house of this period.

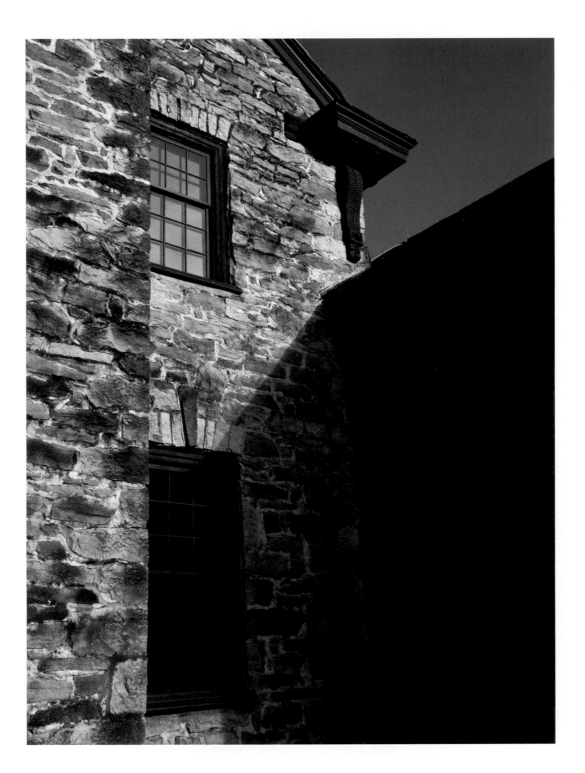

received his medical degree from the University of Pennsylvania, and began his practice in Knoxville and the surrounding counties. He also pursued an active business career, owning several farms, mills, town lots, buildings, and a ferry. At one time or another, he served as trustee for two academies and three colleges, while performing director's duties for a number of railroads and banks. For ten years beginning in 1874, he was president of the Tennessee Historical Society.

But the feat for which J. G. M. Ramsey is most remembered is his authorship of one of the earliest histories of Tennessee. The 744-page book was titled *The Annals of Tennessee to the End of the Eighteenth Century*, more commonly called *Ramsey's Annals*. First published in 1853 in Charleston, South Carolina, the book, according to Alfred Leland Crabb, "is rich in original and previously unpublished matter relating to the experiences of the pioneers [and] contains a vivid account of

Next spread: The Ramsey House Plantation at Swan Pond is located near the confluence of the French Broad and Holston Rivers.

> "Dr. Ramsey [J. G. M. Ramsey] proudly described himself as 'one of the first born of the sons of Tennessee'...and he had the distinction of being the first native-born historian of the state."
>
> Alfred Leland Crabb, 1958

Center hall stairway

the early settlers' participation in the battle of King's Mountain, also the first recorded history of the State of Franklin." Much of Ramey's source material for his book came from his father's journal and personal papers and the memoirs of Isaac Shelby, John Sevier, and William Blount.

Following Colonel Ramsey's death, the house passed to his two sons, J. G. M. Ramsey and William B. A. Ramsey, an early mayor of Knoxville. After their residency, the property was owned by a number of parties and, in time, fell into disrepair. In 1952, the Association for the Preservation of Tennessee Antiquities (APTA) acquired the site and restored the residence and grounds to their early nineteenth-century appearance.

After his residency at the Ramsey House, J. G. M. Ramsey lived at a home he called Mecklenburg, situated at the confluence of the French Broad and Holston Rivers. That home, including Ramsey's valuable library, was destroyed in 1863 by Union troops. After the war, from 1872 until his death, Ramsey resided in a home located at 801 Main Street, S.E., in Knoxville.

Property administered and maintained by the Knoxville Chapter, APTA.

SAM HOUSTON SCHOOLHOUSE

BLOUNT COUNTY

⸺ c. 1794 ⸺

Before Sam Houston led Texas to its independence from Mexico, he taught school in a primitive log cabin situated along Little River in Blount County.

To most Americans, the name Sam Houston (1793–1863) conjures up images of the young soldier-friend of General Andrew Jackson, fighting side by side with him and the Tennessee militia in Alabama during the Creek Wars, or, of the erudite statesman who served as governor of Tennessee during the 1820s, or, more likely than all, of the popularly-elected president of the Republic of Texas following the renegade country's victory over the Mexicans in 1836. But, before all of these important facets of Houston's life, he was simply a young school teacher in East Tennessee, intent on providing educations for his students.

Born in Virginia's Shenandoah Valley, young Samuel, along with his widowed mother and eight siblings, arrived in Blount County, Tennessee, near Maryville, in 1807. Upon his arrival on the frontier, Houston became enamored with the neighboring Cherokee Indians and soon found himself spending protracted periods of time living among them in the wilderness. The Cherokees' respect for the young white man earned him the name "The Raven," which followed him throughout his life.

In Blount County, Houston taught at this primitive schoolhouse originally built by Andrew Kennedy and Henry McCullough. For tuition, Houston charged a yearly fee of eight dollars, but accepted one-third of the fee in corn, one-third in cotton cloth, and the remaining one-third in cash. These were apparently some of the happiest months of Houston's life, and years after his rise to national prominence, he recalled that, "When a young man in Tennessee, I kept a county school…. I experienced a higher feeling of dignity and self-satisfaction than from any office or honor which I have since held." The Sam Houston Schoolhouse is the oldest log school building in Tennessee.

Engraving of Sam Houston as governor of Texas.

Sam Houston Schoolhouse is owned by the State of Tennessee and administered by the Tennessee Historical Commission through the Sam Houston Schoolhouse Association.

CADES COVE

·•· *1818* ·•·

"In 1818, John Oliver walked into a secluded cove high in the mountains, spent the night in an Indian hut, and then tied his life to one of the most beautiful and productive spots in all of Tennessee. This broad, well-watered basin of fertile land was named after the wife of an old Cherokee chief; it was called Kate's Cove, later Cades Cove."

Wilma Dykeman, 1978

For many years before John Oliver laid eyes for the first time upon the pristine beauty of Cades Cove — and even before the widow Martha Huskey Ogle from South Carolina, along with her seven children, settled future Gatlinburg several years earlier — the entire Great Smoky Mountain region of East Tennessee was home to the Cherokees, one of the most powerful Indian tribes ever to inhabit North America. Before white encroachment in the Southern Appalachian region, the Cherokees maintained a number of villages scattered across western North Carolina, East Tennessee, extreme western South Carolina, and northern Georgia. The Tennessee villages were called the Overhill towns and included Chota, Settico, Tellico, and Tannassy (whence Tennessee gets is name).

Soon after pioneer settlement in the region, the proud Cherokees were forced from their mountain fastness to lands far beyond the Mississippi River when Andrew Jackson's Indian Removal Act of 1830 was totally implemented.

Opposite: The Henry and Matilda Whitehead Place, c. 1898, remains as the only square-sawed log home in the Great Smoky Mountains National Park. For this feature, and the rare-for-the-period brick chimney, it is considered a transition house from the early cabins to the frame houses later popular in Cades Cove.

Cades Cove Methodist Church, constructed in 1902, replaced a dirt floor cabin with fire pit, which had served the congregation since the early 1840s. Division during the Civil War and Reconstruction caused dissident members to split off and form the nearby Hopewell Methodist church.

Cades Cove Primitive
Baptist Church,
c. 1887, served a
congregation, which
had existed in the
Cove since 1827.

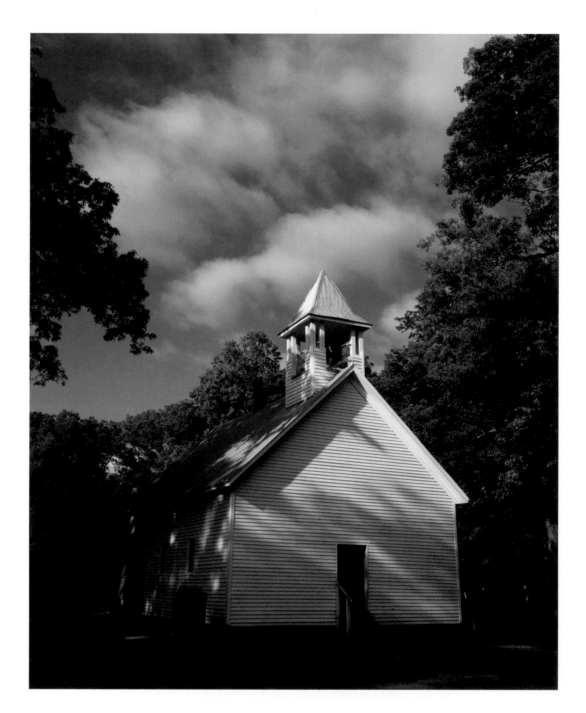

However, a few natives did escape the U.S. Army's forced "Trail of Tears" and retreated into the far reaches of the mountains, where eventually, they became the nucleus for the Qualla Cherokee Indian Reservation located across the Appalachians in North Carolina.

John Oliver's entry into Cades Cove was followed by the appearance of other families whose names still resonate across the region — the Tiptons, Foutes, Gregorys, and Cables. In time, an entire community grew up — numbering 685 residents representing 132 households in 1850 — with families intermarrying with others and propagating future generations of mountain people. Living off the fertile soil, these people grew crops, raised livestock, and became self-sufficient, isolating themselves from the outside world for more than a century. The lifestyles they created for themselves in the remote mountains were reminiscent of that pursued by their Scots-Irish ancestors of eons past.

In addition to their rich cultural heritage prompted by their ancestry and isolation, the first white settlers of the Great Smoky Mountains and Cades Cove were beneficiaries of one of the most bio-diverse regions in the entire world. Within the confines of these mountains are more species of flora and fauna than in the entire continent of Europe.

Cades Cove is preserved much as it was soon after John Oliver and his neighbors cleared the region for agriculture in the early nineteenth century. Homesteads, cabins, mills, and other evidences of pioneer life, some original and some reconstructed, remain. Although John Oliver's cabin was the first residence built in the Cove, the structure visible today nearby the original site was built for his son's honeymoon cabin.

Several churches are present in Cades Cove and were essential to family life. They include traditional frame structures for the Primitive Baptist, Missionary Baptist, and the Methodist congregations, although most were constructed many years after the initial

Headstones in the Primitive Baptist Church Cemetery for John Oliver (1793-1864) and his wife, Lurena Oliver (1795-1888), first permanent settlers of Cades Cove

John Cable Mill on Abrams Creek utilized an overshot wheel to grind meal and power a sawmill, both welcome amenities to the Cades Cove community.

settlement of the area, replacing earlier brush arbors and log meeting houses. Even in the tranquility of Cades Cove, however, religious matters were not without their problems. During the Civil War, the Primitive Baptists and the Missionary Baptists parted ways because as revealed in correspondence of the day, "We [the Primitive Baptists] was Union people and the Rebels was too strong here in Cades Cove."

The largest collection of pioneer buildings in Cades Cove is the Cable Mill complex. All structures there are original to the Great Smoky Mountains, but all except the grist mill were transported to the site from elsewhere in the park. The mill, an example of an early overshot mill, was built by the Cable family early in their settlement of the region. Other examples of early pioneer architecture are a cantilever barn, the Becky Cable house, sorghum mill, corn crib, smokehouse, and blacksmith shop.

In 1904, when Horace Kephart visited the Smoky Mountains for health purposes, he was totally amazed at the vastness and beauty of the region. An avid outdoorsman and conservationist, he visualized that someday the area might be preserved from logging and mining interests as a national park. But others, as early as the 1880s, had already dreamed of the same idea. Eventually, the region did become federally owned thanks to the dedication of many supporters. On September 2, 1940, President Franklin D. Roosevelt presented the park "for the permanent enjoyment of the people."

Becky Cable House – Becky Cable died in this home in 1940 after a productive ninety-four-year life raising the children of two families, farming, tending cattle, and running a boarding house.

Cades Cove from Hyatt Lane, originally an Indian trail

Singing school group,
c. 1901, Primitive
Baptist Church

John McCaulley and
family with load of hay

Luke Lawson,
c. 1915

Milton and Ruby
LeQuire

Next spread: Cades
Cove and Cades
Cove Methodist
Church from Rich
Mountain Road, the
original wagon
road into the Cove
from Tuckaleechee

The U.S. National Park Service administers Cades Cove as part of the Great Smoky Mountains National Park.

NIOTA DEPOT

McMINN COUNTY

1855

The Niota Depot is very likely the oldest surviving railway terminal building in Tennessee.

In early 1836, the Tennessee General Assembly passed legislation incorporating the Hiwassee Railroad Company and giving the company authority to build a line connecting Knoxville with the existing railroad to the south that linked Augusta, Georgia, and Memphis, Tennessee. Work began on the railroad the following year, but after grading only about sixty-five miles of right-of-way, the company went bankrupt. The East Tennessee and Georgia Railroad assumed the work, and in February 1852, the line finally reached the town of Mouse Creek, present-day Niota. The depot was begun during 1854 and opened for use in April 1855. Almost three-and-one-half years later, the rails reached Knoxville, placing Niota in a strategic position along the line.

The sparse military action in the region during the Civil War left the depot unscathed other than for a few bricks being removed from the walls to create firing ports, if such were ever needed. Union General Ambrose Burnside's invasion of East Tennessee in September 1863 resulted locally with a contingent of troops left in the Mouse Creek area. Despite the destruction of miles of track on either side of the depot by Confederate cavalry in August 1864, the railroad remained occupied by the Union army until war's end. In 1869, the East Tennessee and Georgia Railroad changed its name to the East Tennessee, Virginia and Georgia Railroad, and this entity was acquired in 1894 by the Southern Railroad Company, under whose ownership the depot remained until its closing.

The modest depot measures about 112 feet by 42 feet and supports a hipped, cantilevered roof that was originally covered with wooden shingles. Inside was a waiting room, a small ticket office, and space for warehousing freight. The depot served the railroad and the community continuously from its opening until it closed in July 1972. Afterward, it was partially restored and part of it used as offices. The much larger freight and warehouse room remains unaltered.

Among these Niota townspeople gathered at the depot in 1902 are stationmaster James Lafayette Burn (in doorway) and station clerk John L. Forrest (on horseback).

The Niota Depot is owned by the City of Niota and serves as its City Hall.

63

RUGBY VILLAGE
⇥ 1880 ⇤

Rugby's idealistic founder hoped his utopian colony on the Cumberland Plateau would attract young English gentry and teach them to make livings from the soil rather than "starve like gentlemen."

British-born Thomas Hughes (1822–1896) was already a widely read, well-respected writer when he hit upon the idea to organize a colony in the United States for young English gentlemen. Educated at Oxford, Hughes had practiced law, been elected to Parliament twice, and been appointed a Queen's Councilor. In 1857, the publisher Macmillan & Company of London released his *Tom Brown's School Days*, a thinly-veiled autobiography that told of Hughes's own experiences at Rugby School, a respected public institution in England headed by Dr. Thomas Arnold, the father of Matthew Arnold (1822–1888), the noted poet, educator, and critic.

As a young man, Hughes became a disciple of a social/religious movement called Christian Socialism, which had the lofty goal of using Christian doctrine and

Rugby's British founder, Thomas Hughes (1822-1896)

ethics as the tools of social reform. He co-founded the London Working Men's College, serving as its principal for eleven years, organized some of Great Britain's first labor unions, and worked tirelessly for the working masses. The second son of an influential family himself, Hughes knew from first-hand experience the burden under which all but first-born British male heirs were subjected due to the custom of *primogeniture*, which dictated that only first-born males inherit the father's estate. The plight was made even worse by the prevailing social stigma that frowned upon the disinherited children from performing any type of manual labor and by an

Opposite: Christ Church Episcopal, built in 1887, is a fine example of Carpenter Gothic architecture.

Kingstone Lisle, founder Thomas Hughes' house, is based on an "English Rural Style" cottage drawn by famous American architectural designer Andrew Jackson Downing.

economic recession raging in Europe at the time, limiting the number of prestigious jobs available. These non-first-born, unemployed males were to be the beneficiaries of Hughes's grandiose scheme to build an English village in the heart of the Tennessee wilderness.

Using much of the proceeds he had saved from his best-selling book, *Tom Brown's School Days*, Hughes helped organize a corporation that eventually acquired around 40,000 acres of primitive, forested land in Morgan, Scott, and Fentress Counties, a region that had only recently been traversed by a railroad line connecting Cincinnati, Ohio, with Chattanooga, Tennessee. On October 5, 1880, with Hughes in attendance, his Tennessee colony was dedicated amidst much fanfare in both the United States and Great Britain. Within months, buildings were erected, cricket and rugby fields were laid out, and horseback trails were designed. By 1884, the new town of Rugby consisted of seventy beautiful Victorian-style houses and buildings, attracting more than three hundred residents. Philharmonic, dramatic, and literary clubs were organized for the scholarly, while archery, swimming, and tennis competitions kept the athletically inclined busy. A lavishly endowed library housing seven

Hughes originally wrote *Tom Brown's School Days* as a story for his son and was convinced by a friend to have the work published. Printed in more than 170 editions, the book's success provided funding for Hughes to establish Rugby.

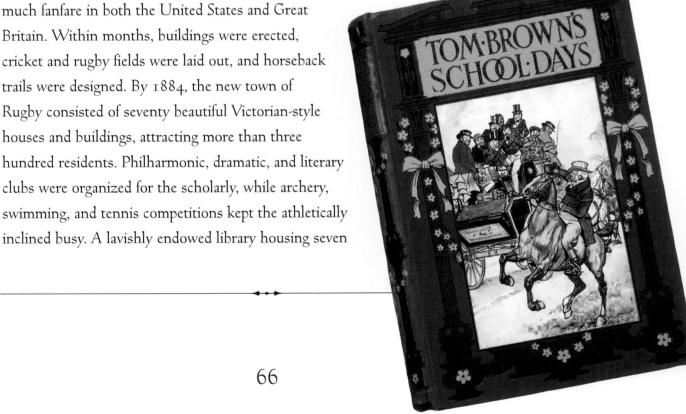

Rugby Schoolhouse, built in 1907

thousand volumes of Victorian-era literature donated by American publishing houses was soon opened. Other structures included an Episcopal church, a hotel named the Tabard Inn after the hostelry in Chaucer's *Canterbury Tales*, butcher shops and general stores, sawmills, and a dairy. Rugby even had its own newspaper.

> *"I can't help feeling and believing that good seed was sown when Rugby was founded and someday the reapers, whoever they may be, will come along with joy bearing heavy sheaves with them."*
>
> Thomas Hughes, 1896

Hughes visited Rugby as often as he could, his responsibilities in England keeping him away much of the time. His mother, brother, and niece all resided there for varying periods. His personal attention, no doubt, had a great impact on the would-be success of the colony, but other factors dealt severe blows to his scheme as well. The year after Rugby opened, a deadly typhoid epidemic visited the Cumberland Plateau, killing seven Rugby residents. Three years later, the Tabard Inn was destroyed by fire. Amidst this misery, finances became strained and Hughes's personal commitment of more than $75,000 was all but gone. But, in the end, one factor above

In 1896, tennis was
a favorite activity
at Rugby.

The Thomas Hughes
Free Public Library
opened in 1882.

Hughes Library interior

Next spread: The Thomas Hughes Library, built in 1882, still has its original 7,000-volume collection intact.

Original library "check-out" cards were written in longhand and bound with string for record-keeping.

all others caused the demise and failure of Rugby. The simple truth was the young gentlemen who populated Rugby did not want to work. In the words of Scott County historian Esther Sanderson, "These young 'aristocrats of the cloth' had no more use for a bull-tongue plow than a razor-backed hog had for a side-saddle. The small effort that this class of gentlemen put forth in clearing the land and tilling the soil was ludicrous."

Although Hughes continued to believe in his ideas and ideals about Rugby, he eventually returned to England for good. His dream lasted less than a decade and, by the turn of the century, Rugby and its environs were well on their way to reverting to the wilderness. During the mid-1960s, the site and several buildings, including the library and its collection, were rescued by area residents and descendants, and by the continuing work of Historic Rugby.

Rugby is administered by the non-profit association, Historic Rugby.

SERGEANT
ALVIN C. YORK MILL
FENTRESS COUNTY
⤙ c. 1880 ⤚

"Fearlessly leading 7 men, he [York] charged with great daring a machinegun nest which was pouring deadly and incessant fire upon his platoon. In this heroic feat the machinegun nest was taken, together with 4 officers and 128 men and several guns."

Citation for Alvin York's Medal of Honor

Congressional Medal of Honor and the French Croix de Guerre awarded to Sgt. York for heroism in France during WWI.

Alvin C. York, arguably one of the most recognized names to emerge from America's World War I experience, was an ordinary Fentress County farmer when he was drafted into the United States army in 1917 upon the nation's entry into the conflict. Born in 1887, York had spent practically his entire life in the county of his birth. In 1914, he had placed membership with the church of Christ in Christian Union, a pacifist denomination; consequently, when he was drafted, he initially requested not to see action. After careful thought, he decided to serve. When isolated behind enemy lines and fiercely attacked by German soldiers, Corporal York took command of his platoon when its leader was killed, and with his followers proceeded to overrun the enemy, killing 25 enemy riflemen and capturing 132 more, as well as 3 machine guns.

York returned home to a hero's welcome and, in 1922, was presented with a brand-new house and a 400-acre farm at Pall Mall, paid for by the Nashville Rotary Club. In 1943, York purchased the circa-1880 gristmill on the nearby Wolf River. He spent the rest of his years on his farm, was the founder of the Alvin C. York Institute for the education of rural children, and dedicated his life to public service. He died in 1964.

York's Mill and the home are now owned by the State of Tennessee and administered by Tennessee State Parks as the Sergeant Alvin C. York State Historic Park.

CRAVENS HOUSE

HAMILTON COUNTY

← 1855 →

Iron-master Robert Cravens never dreamed when he built his house in a bucolic vale half-way up Lookout Mountain that in a few brief years, he and his family would be caught in the crossfire of a great battle between two American armies.

Cravens moved to Ross's Landing in 1838 at about the time the town's name was changed to Chattanooga. When he built his home in 1855, he placed it on a rock outcropping at an altitude of about two thousand feet along the side of Lookout Mountain, overlooking the town and the Tennessee River. The house was a modest one, utilizing two levels, one a basement and the upper, L-shaped one providing living quarters. When the sun was right and the structure was viewed from a distance, it gleamed with a white brilliance and, in time, came to be known as the White House.

The Battle of Chickamauga, fought on September 19 and 20, 1863, provided the Confederate army with its greatest victory in the western theater, but failure to follow up on the retreating Union forces deprived it of Chattanooga, which the Federals occupied immediately. Despite a Confederate siege of the town, Union occupation prevailed, with more than 100,000 troops in the immediate area. From November 23 through 25, 1863, the Union army won engagements on Lookout Mountain and along Missionary Ridge, sending Confederate forces south into Georgia. The Cravens House was in the midst of the conflict on Lookout Mountain —also known as the "Battle above the Clouds" due to the occurrence of a heavy mist that enveloped the mountain—and, although it suffered minor combat damage, wayward Union soldiers later practically demolished it.

Robert Cravens returned after the war and rebuilt his home. When the federal government announced plans to memorialize the Chickamauga-Chattanooga battleground with a military park, Adolph Ochs purchased the property and donated it to the construction effort in 1893.

1903 postcard showing a rebuilt Cravens House, the New York Monument, and the Lookout Mountain Hotel located at the position where Union troops scaled the bluffs forty years earlier

The Cravens House is part of, and is administered by, the Chickamauga-Chattanooga National Military Park.

Craven House, General Walthall's Headquarters, Lookout Mountain.

THE OCHS BUILDING
later named THE DOME BUILDING

◆ *1892* ◆

From the day of its dedication on December 8, 1892, as the new headquarters of The Chattanooga Times, *this building has been one of the city's most iconic and beloved landmarks.*

From the time Adolph Ochs (1858–1935) hired on to his first job at age eleven as office boy for the editor of *The Knoxville Chronicle*, he knew that journalism would be his life's work. His parents were Jewish immigrants from Bavaria, Germany, who had met in Natchez, Mississippi, in 1853, married in Nashville two years later, and eventually settled in Cincinnati, Ohio. Following the Civil War, the Ochs family moved to Knoxville, where young Adolph took a newspaper job to help his parents with expenses. His editor was impressed with his abilities, later recalling that "he [Ochs] swept my sanctum and cleaned up the papers and trash so methodically that he was promoted to delivery boy" at $1.50 per week. After a brief stint with a Louisville, Kentucky, newspaper in his late teens, Ochs returned to Knoxville to take a new job with a startup newspaper, *The Tribune*, where he worked close to two years as a composer, reporter, and assistant to the paper's business manager.

Young Ochs moved to Chattanooga in 1878 to assume a position with *The Chattanooga Daily Dispatch*, just in time to witness the company's failure. Negotiating a deal to acquire the competition, *The Chattanooga Times*, also in financial decline, he eventually rescued the paper and became the sole owner. In late December 1892, he dedicated his new headquarters, the Ochs Building, more often called the Times Building, located at the corner of Georgia

The 25th Anniversary Edition of *The Chattanooga Times* in 1903 contained this Special Edition Supplement.

Avenue and East Eighth Street in downtown Chattanooga. Designed in the Italian Renaissance Revival style by the New York architects A. W. Cordes and Theodore DeLemos, the six-story, stone and brick structure, topped by a gold-gilded, domed cupola—"one of the largest in the country," according to *The Times*—was the

"But his [Ochs's] greatest monument is invisible—the principle of clean, temperate and impartial presentation of news and of higher standards in advertising. These are now such commonplaces of decent newspaper practice that many newspapermen of today may think they have obtained from time immemorial. But they did not secure a foothold easily or automatically; they did not prevail in New York City until Adolph S. Ochs came to town from Chattanooga and risked everything he had on his faith that not only could such a newspaper be published but that there was a public which wanted it."

Adolph Ochs's obituary in *The New York Times*, April 9, 1935

Architectural detail of the magnificent gold-gilded "Dome"

tallest building in town at the time. The morning paper of December 8, 1892, reported that the structure had required for its construction a mind-boggling amount of building materials: 1,600,000 bricks weighing two thousand tons; one hundred tons of lumber; one hundred tons of concrete; 456 tons of iron, including that required for water, steam, and gas pipes; nineteen hundred tons of stone; and four tons of hardware, tin, copper, and sheet-iron.

By then Ochs was enjoying his role as the darling of Chattanooga business circles, at least until the Panic of 1893 drove him to near bankruptcy. By 1896, however, he had survived the economic storm and was attempting to

Adolph S. Ochs, c. 1903, owner and publisher of *The Chattanooga Times*

purchase another small-town journal. He ended up buying a large-city, financially-stressed newspaper, *The New York Times*. Upon the acquisition of *The Times*, Ochs moved permanently to New York City, although he maintained close ties with Chattanooga and its civic leaders. While visiting Chattanooga in April 1935, this business leader and newspaperman *par excellence* passed away.

During the 1920s, the Mountain City Business College, later called the McKenzie College, occupied part of the Ochs Building, along with Western Union offices. In 1947, *The Chattanooga Times* moved to larger quarters and the structure was acquired by new owners who renamed it the Dome Building. Rental offices occupied the building for years, until 1969, when Gordon Street purchased it and, over the next eight years, remodeled and restored it to its original appearance. In 2002, the building was purchased by Greg Vital through the Dome Building Realty Partners, who have recently completed a two-million-dollar renovation and restoration to the property.

Late 19th-century scene of Ochs Building, "*The Chattanooga Times* Building," at East Eighth Street and Georgia Avenue

Property is owned and administered by Dome Building Realty Partners, LLC

TIVOLI
CHATTANOOGA'S
TIVOLI
CHATTANOOGA SYMPHONY
SEASON TICKETS ON SALE NOW
267 8583

TIVOLI THEATRE

⤙ 1921 ⤚

Called the "Jewel of the South" in the 1920s, the Tivoli Theatre brought all the glamour of Hollywood, Broadway, and Vaudeville to a small Southern industrial town.

On the evening of March 19, 1921, the brand new Tivoli Theatre located at 630 Chestnut Street in downtown Chattanooga had its grand opening. The movie that was viewed by hundreds was Cecil B. DeMille's *Forbidden Fruit*, a saga about a poor seamstress whose spendthrift husband depletes all of the family money, leaving the destitute woman to marry a millionaire whom the forlorn husband later attempts to murder, only to be killed himself. Billed that night as "the theatre that will send you away grasping....The wonder theatre," the Tivoli operated for the next forty years as Chattanooga's most popular gathering place for Hollywood movie aficionados.

The Tivoli Theatre was the vision of Frank Dowler Jr., the general manager of the Signal Amusement Company, and it was designed by the world-renowned theater architectural firm of Rapp and Rapp of Chicago. The reported cost of the state-of-the-art building was one million dollars. Beautiful, yet unpretentious on

The Tivoli marquee as it appeared during the inaugural 1921 season

the outside, the theater's cavernous interior was nothing short of opulent. Gold-plated chandeliers, ornamental plasterwork, an awesome staircase, a high coffered ceiling, luxurious velvet curtains, and multi-colored stage lights all added to the Beaux Arts design that was so popular at the time in movie houses across the United States.

Over the years visitors to a movie at the Tivoli could be

assured that they would get their money's worth. Main features included such popular films as *One Night of Love*, starring native-Tennessean Grace Moore; the blockbuster *Gone With the Wind*, with Clark Gable, Vivien Leigh, and a stellar cast; *Dodsworth*, featuring Walter Huston; and *Under Two Flags*, with Ronald Colman and Claudette Colbert. Besides the movie, the viewer was also treated with newsreels of current events, cartoons, and most times, a several-minute travelogue or other special feature.

"Here is a shrine to democracy where there are no privileged patrons. The wealthy rub elbows with the poor—and are better for this contact. Do not wonder, then, at the touches of Italian Renaissance…or at the lobbies and foyers…. These are no impractical attempts at showing off. These are part of a celestial city—a cavern of many colored jewels, where iridescent lights and luxurious fittings heighten the expectations of pleasure. It is richness unabashed, but richness with a reason."

George Rapp, of the architectural firm of Rapp and Rapp, 1925

By August 17, 1961, the popularity of television and a decline in moviegoers made for dwindling revenues at the Tivoli and other movie theaters across the country. The final performance, *Snow White and the Three Stooges*, was watched by a few die-hard movie-goers before the curtain fell for the last time. Fortunately for theater-lovers and historic preservationists alike, the old building was rescued when the City of Chattanooga, the Greater Chattanooga Chamber of Commerce, and the property owner came to an agreement whereby the city leased the theater and assigned its oversight to the Memorial Auditorium/Tivoli Theatre Board, with the provision that movies not be shown to avoid competition with the owner's other movie houses in the city.

The Tivoli's second grand opening was performed before a sold-out house on March 5, 1963, with a

Poster for "Forbidden Fruit," the first movie to play at the new Tivoli

formal dedication followed by a concert by the Chattanooga Symphony Orchestra. Thirteen years later, when the City of Chattanooga purchased the Tivoli for $300,000, movies were brought back once again (the first showing was *High Noon*, starring Gary Cooper and Grace Kelly). A multi-year study was soon launched to determine how best to adapt the theater to the needs of the late twentieth century. With grant money from the Lyndhurst Foundation and planning assistance from Chattanooga Venture, a $5.5-million overhaul was proposed, and, with funding provided by the Tennessee General Assembly, the

The most glamorous event of the 1930s was the September 1934 southern premiere of "One Night of Love," starring Tennessean Grace Moore, the internationally acclaimed opera star and daughter of Colonel and Mrs. Richard Moore, owners of Loveman's Department Store.

City of Chattanooga, and private donors, the money was raised, and renovation began in June 1987. Nearly two years later, the old theater reopened once again and, this time, to its original splendor.

The soaring gold-leaf opulence of the Tivoli's loge seats

The Tivoli Theatre is owned by the City of Chattanooga and administered by the Tivoli-Auditorium Promotion Association (TAPA).

CRAGFONT
SUMNER COUNTY
→ *1802* ←

Today, sadly, James Winchester remains largely forgotten and his place in Tennessee history is overshadowed by more notable, yet sometimes less accomplished, men.

With a little imagination, a present-day visitor to Cragfont can readily visualize how the surrounding countryside must have appeared more than two hundred years ago when James Winchester completed his magnificent house atop a forested bluff overlooking Bledsoe's Creek. Approaching the stately structure along the long drive leading from present-day Tennessee Highway 25E, once part

of the old Holston Road connecting Nashville and Knoxville, one can almost hear the sounds of the once-thick wilderness in which Winchester chose to build.

Winchester had arrived in the region with his brother George in 1785 and had built his first home, a log structure, on the site shortly afterward. Born in Maryland in 1752, James had served with distinction in the Revolution, been taken prisoner twice, and witnessed the British surrender to General George Washington at Yorktown in October 1781. He fared well in the Cumberland settlements and, within a few years, had acquired hundreds of acres of prime land, married Susan Black, sired several children, and, upon Tennessee's admission to the Union in 1796, was appointed brigadier-general of the militia and elected speaker of the state senate.

For the times and the location, Winchester's vision of Cragfont was truly amazing. Even in 1798, the year he began construction, Middle Tennessee was still on the far reaches of the frontier. It had been only a dozen years since Sumner

Portrait of James Winchester painted by Ralph E. W. Earl in 1817 when Winchester was 65 years old

89

County had been organized and just four years since Winchester's brother George, while en route to Gallatin, was killed by Indians. The French naturalist, François André Michaux, traveled the Cumberland region during September 1802, and later commented upon the nearly completed Cragfont.

> *We likewise saw, en passant, General Winchester, who was at a stone house that was building for him on the road; this mansion, considering the country, bore the external marks of grandeur; it consisted of four large rooms on the ground floor, one story, and a garret.*

What could have been more magnificent for the times—when most folks in the region were content with abodes of logs, clapboard, and in a few instances, brick—than a home built of dressed, local limestone and crafted by skilled masons? Whatever was the reasoning behind Winchester's dream, the final product was— and is to this day—one of Tennessee's most splendid properties. The first level of the front section of the house consists of a massive central hallway, with a single parlor to the left and a smaller parlor and music room to the right. Above these rooms on the second level are four bedrooms. Large chimneys on either end of the

ROCK CASTLE

SUMNER COUNTY

⟶ *1784–1791* ⟵

"The General [Smith] is possessed of a splendid estate which is cultivated in cotton and maize. America is indebted to him for the best map of the state.... He spends his leisure moments in the study of chemistry."

François André Michaux, 1805

Daniel Smith (1748–1818) was one of the most influential leaders on the Tennessee frontier. A surveyor by profession, he attended William and Mary College in Williamsburg, served in both Lord Dunmore's War and the American Revolution, and surveyed the Virginia-North Carolina boundary—all before migrating to present-day Sumner County around 1783. In his new home, he assumed positions of importance, among them trustee of Davidson Academy, brigadier-general of the Mero District militia, secretary of the Southwest Territory upon its formation in 1790, and, soon after Tennessee attained statehood in 1796, United States senator. His 1794 map of present-day Tennessee is the earliest depiction of the state as a stand-alone entity.

Smith's two-story home, Rock Castle, was begun in 1784, a task which required seven years to complete, primarily due to Indian unrest. Situated on an original land grant of 3,140 acres, the seven-room house is built of dressed, locally quarried limestone and is a blending of Georgian and Federal architecture. Since no stone workers were available in the Cumberland River Valley at the time, masons for the job were brought in from Lexington, Kentucky. Before completion, seven of them were killed by the natives.

Daniel Smith, a surveyor and territorial secretary for territorial governor William Blount, was commissioned to create this early map and is credited for first using "Tennessee" as a name for the new state.

During the 1950s, the waters of Old Hickory Lake engulfed a large part of Rock Castle's original acreage, and today, the house, a family cemetery, and a smokehouse reside on the remaining eighteen acres.

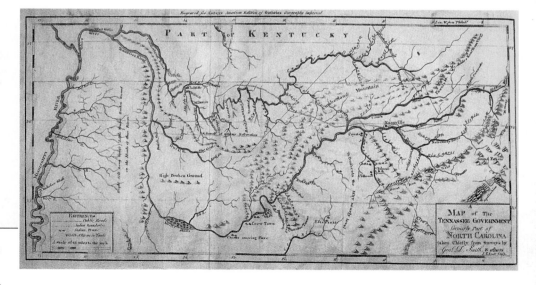

Rock Castle is owned by the State of Tennessee and administered by the Tennessee Historical Commission through the Friends of Rock Castle.

93

CAIRO ROSENWALD SCHOOL

⟶ 1923 ⟵

A proud African-American community in Sumner County contributed cash and in-kind donations of material and labor to match the Rosenwald Fund's generous support in building a school for their children.

The Cairo Rosenwald School, located in the Cairo community near Gallatin, was built in 1923 with support from the Julius Rosenwald Fund, which had already helped to build hundreds of similar schools for African-American children across the South. Booker T. Washington and other black educators earlier had persuaded Julius Rosenwald, president of the giant retailer, Sears, Roebuck and Company, and founder of the Julius Rosenwald Fund, to donate funds for the construction of well-designed rural schools for African Americans as long as fund-raising within the black community at least matched— and typically residents far exceeded—the money from the Rosenwald Fund.

The first six "Rosenwald" schools were built in rural Alabama, but before the giant program ceased operations in 1932, nearly five thousand schools, 217 teachers' homes, and 163 shop buildings serving 883 counties in fifteen states had been erected at a cost of nearly thirty million dollars. By 1928, one out of five schools serving black children in the South was funded by the Julius Rosenwald Fund, which

Julius Rosenwald, Founder of the Rosenwald Fund.

A teacher and her students were photographed next to the first school building for African American students in Cairo (c. 1910).

was based in Nashville for much of its history (1920–1932). Tennesseans built 350 Rosenwald Fund-supported facilities.

Cairo Rosenwald School is typical of many of these Tennessee buildings—a framed one-room school with a bank of tall windows on the west side providing light for the inside. But the experiences and memories of the students who were educated within these walls remind us of differences between today and the mid-twentieth century past. Verdell Williams told *USA Today* on April 7, 2008, about her first school day in 1938. "About 30 of us, all eight grades. My teacher was Mrs. Loretta McMurray Young. She was very nice, but very strict. She had boys in there bigger than she was, but she didn't have any problems. She had a little hickory stick. Back then, you could whip the kids. They wouldn't go home and tell it because they knew they would just get another whipping."

African Americans contributed labor, materials, and $700 for the school's construction while the Rosenwald Fund added the architectural plans and $500. The Tennessee public school fund contributed $700. These funds built a school that served local children until 1959. The schoolhouse was restored and renovated in 2008–2009, with grant funds from the Lowe's Charitable and Educational Foundation and the National Trust for Historic Preservation. The MTSU Center for Historic Preservation and the Tennessee Preservation Trust assisted in acquiring the funds.

Cairo Rosenwald School student body along with the superintendent of schools and John Hutch Brinkley, teacher (c. 1950)

The annual Easter Sunday Morning Community breakfast at Cairo School (c. 1948)

Teacher, John Hutch Brinkley, and his students (c. 1953) on the front steps of the school

Second and third grade boys engaged in physical education class (c. 1948)

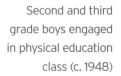

Cairo Rosenwald School is owned and operated by the Cairo Improvement Club as a community center.

SAM DAVIS HOME

⟶ 1810–1850 ⟵

The tragic story of a young Southern hero is memorialized on the grounds of his boyhood home.

In the annals of American military history, Sam Davis, often called "the Boy Hero of the Confederacy," has been compared to Revolutionary War icon Nathan Hale, both hanged by enemy forces for refusing to divulge critical intelligence. Davis was born in Rutherford County in 1842, raised on the family farm near Smyrna, and attended the Western Military Institute in Nashville. Enlisting in the 1st Tennessee Infantry Regiment at the beginning of the Civil War, young Davis soon saw action with General Robert E. Lee during the Cheat Mountain campaign in western Virginia (present-day West Virginia). During 1862, the 1st Tennessee, with Davis on hand, participated in skirmishes at Shiloh and Perryville, ending the year at Murfreesboro, where, a few days later, Confederate General Braxton Bragg's Army of Tennessee retreated southward.

During 1863, Sam Davis rode with Coleman's Scouts, a small, localized unit whose primary mission was to disrupt Union communication lines throughout Middle Tennessee. In late November, near Minor Hill in Giles County, Davis was captured by elements of General Grenville Dodge's command and taken to nearby Pulaski. Convinced that Davis was a spy by the presence on his person of several documents revealing recent troop movements in the area, Union officers demanded that the young man reveal the source of the papers. When Sam refused, he was court-martialed, found guilty of being a courier and a spy, and sentenced to hang. Just prior to his execution near the Pulaski Public Square on November 27, 1863, he is reported to have declared, "If I had a thousand lives, I would lose them all here before I would betray my friend or the confidence of my informer."

Photo of Sam Davis (left) and his brother, John, made just prior to the war, possibly wearing the uniform of Nashville's Western Military Institute, which became Montgomery Bell Academy. Photo courtesy of Sam Davis Memorial Association.

Slave cabins with cotton fields awaiting harvest at the Davis plantation

Sam's body was returned to his parents' home where he was interred in the family cemetery behind the house. His epitaph reads:

He Laid Down His Life for His Country,
A Truer Soldier, a Purer Patriot, a Braver Man
Never Lived. He Suffered Death on the Gibbet
Rather than Betray His Friends and Country.

The first phase of Sam Davis's childhood home near Smyrna was built along Stewart's Creek in 1820 by Moses Ridley, an early settler of Nashville, who also built the nearby, almost identical, Ridley-Buchanan House. In time, Sam's parents, Charles Lewis and Jane Simmons Davis, acquired the property, raised cotton, and, in 1850, extensively renovated and remodeled their home to its present appearance. The two-story, framed I-house with Greek Revival portico contains nine rooms and

"Dear Mother: O how painful it is to write you! I have got to die tomorrow—
to be hanged by the Federals. Mother, do not grieve for me. I must bid you
good-bye forevermore. Mother, I do not fear to die. Give my love to all.
—Your dear son, Sam."

sits upon the remaining 168 acres of the original Ridley land grant. The kitchen,
an overseer's office, a smokehouse, and several restored slave dwellings (not
original to the site) rest nearby. Many of the furnishings in the home are original,
as are much of the interior woodwork, doors, and floors.

The State of Tennessee purchased the Davis property in 1927, restored and
renovated it, and opened it to the public in 1930.

The Sam Davis Home is administered by the Sam Davis Memorial Association.

OAKLANDS

— c. 1818 first phase —
— 1857–1860 present-day appearance —

Prominent visitors to Oaklands include C.S.A. President Jefferson Davis; the "Pathfinder of the Seas," Commodore Matthew Fontaine Maury; presidential candidate John Bell; Mrs. James K. Polk; and Confederate Generals Braxton Bragg and Leonidas Polk.

Its genesis was a simple two-room, one-and-a-half-story brick house begun around 1818, but over the ensuing years, Oaklands grew into one of Tennessee's most successful and productive plantations. In 1813, Sallie Murfree, daughter of Murfreesboro's namesake, Colonel Hardee Murfree, inherited 274 acres of land in town where she and her husband, Dr. James Maney, decided to build their home and raise their family. The structure was enlarged during the 1820s and again in the 1830s, as more children came along. During the late 1850s, following Sallie Maney's death and Dr. Maney's retirement, the stately mansion was inherited by the Maneys' son, Lewis, and his wife, Rachel Cannon, daughter of former Tennessee governor, Newton Cannon, who hired local architect Richard Sanders to add the prominent Italianate features and window treatments visible in the house today.

Gen. Nathan Bedford Forrest

During mid-July 1862, General Nathan Bedford Forrest and his command raided Union-held Murfreesboro and skirmished extensively with the 9th Michigan Infantry Regiment. Forrest accepted the Union surrender of the town in one of the front rooms of Oaklands. Murfreesboro was then held by the Confederates until year's end, when, once again, the Union army occupied the entire region as a result of the Battle of Stones River.

Saved from demolition and the spawning of a public housing project in its place during the late 1950s, present-day Oaklands is a prime example of historic preservation at its best.

Oaklands is owned and operated by the Oaklands Association.

THE HERMITAGE

DAVIDSON COUNTY

~ *1836* ~

The Hermitage is the fourth most visited presidential residence in the United States, surpassed only by the White House, Mount Vernon, and Monticello.

In 1788, when Andrew Jackson (1767–1845), a tall, lanky, red-haired youth, rode into Nashville with a satchel full of law books and little else to assume his new job as public prosecutor in Judge John McNairy's court, the furthest thought from his mind was that, one day, he would be elected president of the United States. At the time, he had more important issues to consider, among them whether or not he would eventually make his permanent home in the small, eight-year-old town on the banks of the Cumberland River. His marriage three years later to Rachel Donelson Robards (1767–1828), the daughter of Nashville's co-founder John Donelson, settled the question.

Five years after the wedding, the Jacksons settled into their new plantation called Hunter's Hill, located about two miles from the future Hermitage. In 1804, Jackson disposed of Hunter's Hill and purchased the nearby Hermitage property from Nathaniel Hayes. He and Rachel moved into the existing two-story, log blockhouse on the site and named the property, first Rural Retreat, and shortly afterward, the Hermitage, where they lived until 1821, when a new two-story, eight-room home was completed on the site. Jackson rapidly expanded his land holdings to one thousand acres, tended by forty-four slaves. By now, he had already become an American icon following the defeat of the Creek Indians in

This Ralph E. W. Earl portrait was one of several he painted of President Jackson in the White House between 1834 and 1836.

Alabama in 1813 and his decisive victory over the British army at New Orleans in early 1815.

In the election of 1828, Jackson was elected president of the United States, but as he prepared to leave Nashville for the inauguration in March, Rachel died, leaving the hero of New Orleans totally devastated. In 1831, while serving as chief executive, he had the Hermitage remodeled, added additional space, and had erected a proper monument in the gardens over Rachel's gravesite. Three years after the remodeling, a fire swept through the mansion and literally destroyed the entire structure.

Undaunted, President Jackson hired the Nashville architects and builders Joseph Reiff and William C. Hume to rebuild the Hermitage in the imposing Greek Revival design that is visible today. The restoration was completed in 1836 in time for Jackson's homecoming from Washington D.C. the following year. He lived there until his death in 1845.

The Hermitage Church on the Hermitage grounds, built by Jackson in honor of his wife, Rachel

Andrew Jackson, Jr., Andrew and Rachel's adopted son, inherited the Hermitage following President Jackson's death. Jackson, Jr., soon began disposing of the Hermitage property and, by 1853, he had mortgaged the entire estate. He sold the mansion and five hundred acres of the plantation in 1856 to the State of

Tennessee and moved to Mississippi. Over the next several years, various plans were discussed for preservation of the Hermitage, including the establishment of a southern branch of the United States Military Academy, an executive mansion for the governor of Tennessee, and a public school. None came to fruition.

Eventually, in 1889, the Ladies' Hermitage Association (LHA) was organized and orchestrated the acquisition of the Hermitage mansion, gardens, and outbuildings. The remaining acreage was devoted to the construction of the Confederate Soldiers' Home to be located on the other side of the Nashville-Lebanon Pike. Following the demise of the soldiers' home in 1933, its acreage reverted to the LHA, who over the years since, has acquired not only Andrew Jackson's total Hermitage holdings when he died—some 1,050 acres—but seventy additional acres. Together, the 1,120 acres administered by the LHA include the Hermitage Wildlife Management Area.

When Jackson died in 1845, he was laid to rest beside his beloved Rachel in the Hermitage gardens, which were designed at his request by the renowned Philadelphia horticulturalist William Frost during the construction of the 1821 Hermitage. Today, the 1836 Hermitage, the gardens, and the surrounding countryside, still appear much as they were during Jackson's residency, despite a savage tornado that struck the Hermitage grounds in 1998, sparing the buildings but destroying hundreds of ancient trees planted by Jackson himself.

This log farmhouse was the Jackson family's home at the Hermitage plantation until 1821, when they moved into the newly completed mansion.

Property administered by the Ladies' Hermitage Association

"Mrs. Jackson chose the spot.... The house was built
in the secluded meadow."

Attributed to Andrew Jackson, by Marquis James, in *Andrew Jackson, the Border Captain*, 1933

The Tomb of President Andrew Jackson and Rachel is set in a peaceful corner of Rachel's Garden and at the edge of the Hermitage's bucolic meadows.

Locket carried by Jackson with a portrait of his beloved wife, Rachel

TULIP GROVE
⟶ 1836 ⟵

*Andrew and Rachel Jackson's favorite nephew had this
architectural jewel built for his wife as a wedding gift.*

It is said that President Martin Van Buren, successor to President Andrew
Jackson, suggested the name for the lovely Greek Revival mansion set in a grove of
tulip poplar trees across the Nashville-Lebanon Pike from Jackson's Hermitage.
Built by Andrew Jackson Donelson, Old Hickory's presidential secretary and a
nephew of Jackson's late wife, Rachel, the home was a belated wedding gift to his
wife, Emily. Early on in Jackson's first administration, Donelson and wife, Emily,
served their kinsman well, Emily serving as Jackson's "First Lady." However, when
the "Peggy Eaton Affair" surfaced, threatening the dissolution of Jackson's entire
cabinet, the Donelsons bid farewell to Washington D.C. and returned to Tennessee.

Tulip Grove was set on more than one thousand acres of prime farmland and
consisted of thirteen rooms. The entrance hall was decorated with murals painted by
the celebrated artist, Ralph E. W. Earl. Completed at a cost of a little over six
thousand dollars, its walls contain 150,000 bricks. Unfortunately, the Donelsons
called it home for only a few months before Emily died of tuberculosis.

A few years later, Donelson married Elizabeth Randolph, the widow of
Thomas Jefferson's grandson, and the couple lived at Tulip Grove. In the
meantime, Donelson continued his involvement in national affairs and was
appointed by President John Tyler as the *charge d'affaires* to the Republic of Texas
and, later, given the post of minister to Prussia by President James K. Polk. In
1856, on the "Know-Nothing" Party ticket, Donelson, as a running mate to Millard
Fillmore, vied unsuccessfully for the office of vice-president of the United States.

The Donelsons sold Tulip Grove in 1858 and moved to Memphis. Since then,
several families have maintained the mansion, the last being the Buntins. In the
early 1960s, the house and sixty surrounding acres were purchased by the Ladies'
Hermitage Association. Another historic site located nearby is the Confederate
Cemetery containing the graves of 483 Confederate veterans, most of whom died at
the neighboring Confederate Soldiers' Home.

Portraits of Andrew
Jackson Donelson
and his wife, Emily
Donelson, Jackson's
"First Lady," likely
painted during the
Jackson presidency

The Ladies' Hermitage Association administers Tulip Grove.

TENNESSEE STATE CAPITOL

— 1859 —

As one of the oldest working capitols in the United States, the Tennessee State Capitol houses the tomb of its architect and is the burial site of a U. S. president. In the past it served as a Civil War fort, and witnessed the final ratifying vote for woman suffrage.

Nashville was the last of four Tennessee communities to serve as the state's capital and seat of government. Upon its formation in 1796, the state administered its affairs from Knoxville, followed by Kingston, Knoxville again, Nashville, Knoxville again, Murfreesboro, and finally Nashville once again. As dictated by the new state constitution of 1834, the 1843 General Assembly chose Nashville, with a population of between seven and eight thousand, as the permanent capital. The first meeting place for state government in Nashville was a small building located at present-day Eighth Avenue and Broad Street.

Two years following Nashville's selection, plans were released for a magnificent new capitol building, to be designed and built by famed Philadelphia architect William Strickland, a student of Benjamin Latrobe and the winner of the design competition. Strickland was eminently qualified for the task, having already produced such worthy projects as Philadelphia's Masonic Temple, as well as the city's U. S. Customs House. Arriving in Nashville in 1845, he could not have known that his work on the Tennessee State Capitol would take the rest of his life, as well as a major involvement on the part of his son, Francis W. Strickland.

The city's site selection committee chose a high hill called Campbell's Knob paralleling Cedar Street (present-day Charlotte Avenue) between High (Sixth Avenue) and Vine (Seventh Avenue) Streets as its choice for the building. Nashville Judge George Washington Campbell had acquired the property years earlier as

William Strickland, architect for the State Capitol, is entombed within its walls.

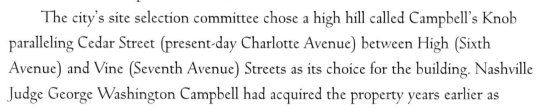

FISK JUBILEE HALL

DAVIDSON COUNTY

—— *1876* ——

During the early days of Fisk University, the Jubilee Singers lifted their voices during a world tour to support the financially struggling institution. Their success created a rich cultural heritage that has become an important part of Nashville's history.

Shortly after the Civil War, concern arose across the United States over the quality of educational opportunities being afforded the recently freed slaves. Within months following the hostilities, officials of the American Missionary Association of New York and the Western Freedman's Aid Commission of Cincinnati decided that Nashville would be an appropriate site for a school of higher learning for freed Negroes who desired to continue their education. At the time, Clinton B. Fisk (1828–1890), a New York-born, Michigan-raised businessman, who had served in the Civil War as a Union army brigadier general fighting Confederate units in Arkansas and Missouri, was the head of the Freedmen's Bureau of Tennessee. With his assistance, on January 9, 1866, Fisk School, named in his honor, was

Fourteen-foot portrait of the first Jubilee Singers painted by the Queen's court painter Edmund Havell, Jr., while the singers were in London.

The original Fisk Jubilee Singers, c. 1871, embarked on a successful national tour before adding two members and touring Europe.

"With 'Steal Away,' 'Roll, Jordan, Roll,' 'Go Down, Moses,' and 'Flee as a Bird to Our Mountain,' they furnished the bricks and the mortar, the stone and wood, the ornamental iron, the copper boilers for steam heat and the wages of the laborers who dug its foundations deep into solid blue stone or installed the mahogany wainscoting that came from the Mendi Mission in South Africa."

Clara Hieronymus, 1966, on the occasion of Fisk University's one-hundredth anniversary.

opened in Nashville. The following year, the school was officially chartered as Fisk University and so it remains today.

Money was tight in those inflationary days after the war and operational expenses took every penny. In 1871, George L. White, the school's treasurer, came up with an idea that not only raised enough money to save the institution, but also created a legend that continues to this day. He organized a nine-member group of singers—men and women—whom he visualized would go on tour singing "slave songs." White soon named the group the "Jubilee Singers," referencing the year of the Jubilee referred to in the Book of Leviticus, Chapter 25. One of the early concerts in Cincinnati grossed $50, but the money, rather than going back to Nashville to help with the school's finances, was instead donated to victims of the famous 1871 Chicago fire.

The novelty of Negro gospel music caught on rapidly and the Jubilee Singers soon embarked on a nationwide tour. In 1872, they attended the World Peace Festival in Boston and performed for President Ulysses S. Grant at the White House. The following year, the group was enlarged by two members, toured England and the Continent, and sang before such notables as Queen Victoria, Prime Minister Gladstone, and Kaiser William of Germany. While in London, the singers—seven women and four men—were memorialized in a giant, ten-by-fourteen-foot painting by the Queen's court painter Edmund Havell, Jr., and the portrait is presently displayed in Jubilee Hall.

The 1949 edition of the Fisk Jubilee Singers performed in commemoration of the famed 1873 European tour and command performance for Queen Victoria.

With the income from the highly successful European tour, school officials purchased the twenty-five-acre site once occupied by Fort Gillem, a Union army redoubt in North Nashville, and authorized construction of Fisk's first permanent building, Jubilee Hall. The massive, Victorian-Gothic-design structure, built of "the best pressed brick with stone trimmings," contained 120 rooms. Dedication ceremonies were held on January 1, 1876, and were attended by General Fisk and many local dignitaries.

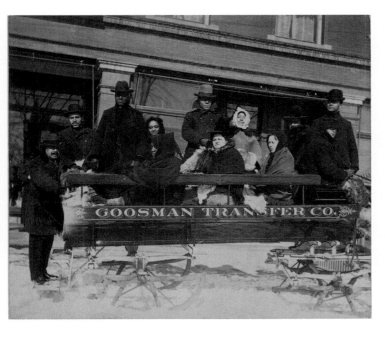

Fisk Jubilee Singers, c. 1901

By the 1950s, although Jubilee Hall's exterior had fared well, its interior had fallen into disrepair, raising serious questions and heated debates over whether to demolish the building. Cooler heads prevailed and in 1955, the building's interior was remodeled. During 1984, with funding from the U.S. Department of the Interior, Jubilee Hall underwent an "historic rehabilitation."

Jubilee Hall is a monument to a small group of dedicated men and women who, when times were tough and the future of their school was uncertain, rose above the challenges and emerged victorious.

RYMAN AUDITORIUM

DAVIDSON COUNTY

1892

It would be a major feat to identify a building in the United States that has played host to a more varied list of performers, evangelists, entertainers, and speech-makers than the Ryman Auditorium. The names read like a "Who's Who" of Americana—President Theodore Roosevelt, Arctic explorer Admiral Robert E. Peary, Booker T. Washington, W. C. Fields, composer Victor Herbert, Helen Keller, the Fisk Jubilee Singers, Rudolph Valentino, Ethel Barrymore, Miriam Anderson, Orson Welles, Helen Hayes, Hank Williams, Doris Day, Will Rogers—the list goes on and on.

On May 10, 1885, as fast-living Nashville riverboat captain Thomas G. Ryman (1841–1904) sat enthralled in the audience of evangelist Sam Jones's fire-and-brimstone sermon, he decided then and there to become a Christian, and from that day forward, he dedicated his life to religion. He visualized the building of a great tabernacle, devoted to serve as a place where itinerant evangelists, such as Jones, could hold revivals, preach, and convert wayward souls to follow the true path. In 1892, following four years of construction, Ryman's dream came true when his Union Gospel Tabernacle on Summer Street (present-day Fifth Avenue North) was completed with a seating capacity of 3,755.

Nashville architect Hugh Cathcart Thompson designed the building with Gothic Revival exterior detailing. Erected in the form of a two-and-one-half-story rectangle, the building measured 120 feet wide by 178 feet deep. The foundation was rock-faced limestone coursed ashlar and rock-faced limestone coursed rubble. The exterior walls were of brick masonry, with limestone and metal detailing. The roof was covered with asphalt shingles. The interior consisted of framing and walls covered with plaster. Floors were of pine. Concentric rows of benches faced the

Opposite: The "Confederate Gallery" balcony was added to the Ryman Tabernacle to accommodate the thousands of Confederate veterans expected in Nashville for the 1897 Confederate Veterans' Reunion.

Grand Ole Opry microphone

pulpit. In 1897, the Confederate Gallery was added, expanding the seating capacity to six thousand, making the tabernacle the largest assembly hall in the South. The gallery was reached by a grand staircase. A large stage built in 1901 to accommodate the New York Metropolitan Opera's productions of *Carmen*, *The Barber of Seville*, and *Faust* reduced the seating capacity back to around 3,500.

"There have been many other colorful steamboat men on the Cumberland, but it is doubtful if any surpassed Tom Ryman. He was known in all the business and social circles of Nashville, and was…beloved by the poor and underprivileged whom he always helped. In the waning years of his life, assisting and encouraging the needy became an obsession…. He had a way of making rough men, cursing men and drinking men quiet down. He called a spade a spade and a crook a crook. He was fearless, sober, honest and, as one of his close friends said, 'gave more to life than he took away with it.'"

Byrd Douglas, 1961, in *Steamboatin' on the Cumberland*

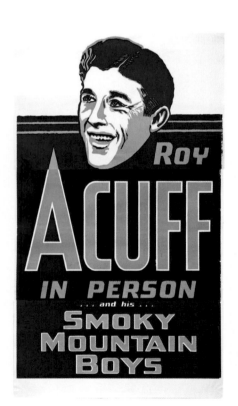

When Captain Ryman died in 1904, Reverend Sam Jones returned to Nashville to preach his funeral. During the ceremony, he asked for votes to decide whether to rename the tabernacle, the Ryman Auditorium. A standing ovation from those assembled decided the question and, until 1963, when the National Life and Accident Insurance Company purchased the building and renamed it the Grand Ole Opry House, it was known by that name.

For years, the Ryman played host to hundreds of American entertainment, political, and religious venues, including grand operas, plays, funerals, orchestra recitals, political speeches, cultural

Original, hand-crafted posters created by Hatch Show Print promoting the Grand Ole Opry at the Ryman Auditorium in the early 1940s. Hatch Show Print is perhaps the oldest continuously operating letterpress and design shop in America, and is administered by the Country Music Hall of Fame.

programs, and just about anything else that required a large seating capacity. In mid-1943, the world-famous Grand Ole Opry moved to the building and utilized it until 1974, when the show relocated to its new Opry House at Opryland USA. Once threatened with demolition, local preservationists, in a nationally publicized movement, rallied to save the building.

In 1993, the Grand Ole Opry's owners, Gaylord Entertainment, initiated an $8,500,000 renovation of the property, and the following year, the building reopened as the Ryman Auditorium. Billed as a performance hall and museum, it soon earned the title, the "Carnegie Hall of the South." In 2001, the Ryman was declared a National Historic Landmark.

Union Gospel Tabernacle, c. 1890s, on Summer Street (present-day Fifth Avenue North)

Minnie Pearl

Dave Macon and Sam

Grand Ole Opry audience c. 1950s

A very young Porter Wagoner performing on the Grand Ole Opry stage.

Ryman Auditorium, owned and operated by Gaylord Attractions, serves as a concert hall and frequent host for Grand Ole Opry performances.

DOWNTOWN PRESBYTERIAN CHURCH
Organized as the First Presbyterian Church

DAVIDSON COUNTY

1851

"The Downtown Presbyterian Church…remains the largest and best preserved example of Egyptian Revival Architecture in America's church buildings."

Dr. J. E. Windrow, 1971

The First Presbyterian Church in Nashville was chartered on the Public Square in 1814 by six women and one man. Reverend Gideon Blackburn of Franklin assisted in the organization and within two years a building was raised on the corner of present-day Fifth Avenue and Church Street, the site where the congregation met for

the next one hundred and thirty-nine years. The simple building was destroyed by
fire in 1832 and replaced by a more elaborate one, seating one thousand people and
erected at a cost of $30,000. In 1848, flames claimed this structure as well, and the
present building superseded it, being dedicated on Easter Sunday, 1851.

William Strickland, the prominent Philadelphia architect responsible for the
Tennessee State Capitol, was selected to design the church, and his exotic plans
reflected the strong, current interest in the United States for all things Egyptian. The
twin-towered structure with its prevalent Egyptian-inspired doors and windows is one
of about sixty such examples of Egyptian Revival architecture dating to the period.
The church's highly decorated and richly embellished interior dates from the 1880s.

Over the years, many of Nashville's notables have attended the First
Presbyterian Church, including Mrs. Rachel Jackson, Mrs. James K. Polk, Felix
Grundy, John Bell, Alfred Hume, Philip and John Berrien Lindsley, and Howell E.
Jackson, among others. During the Civil War, the church was utilized as a Union
hospital. In 1955, the Downtown congregation moved to a new building on
Franklin Road, while many dissident members stayed
behind to organize the present-day Downtown Presbyterian
Church in the time-hallowed building on the original site.

Civil War-era photograph
of First Presbyterian
Church at Church and
Fifth Streets, made during
the Union occupation

BELLE MEADE
DAVIDSON COUNTY
farm—1807, house—1853

Thoroughbred studs standing at Belle Meade during the latter half of the 19th century were the progenitors of many champion racehorses of the modern era, including Northern Dancer and Triple Crown winner, Secretariat.

Before Belle Meade, the plantation was the small frontier fort called Dunham's Station. Built in the early 1780s by the Dunham family on the small bluff overlooking Richland Creek west of Nashville, the dog-trot log cabin was but one of many such defensive structures that protected the region's first settlers from hostile Indians.

Virginia-born John Harding, a Thoroughbred breeder and racing aficionado, established Belle Meade Farm, the "Queen of Tennessee Plantations," in 1807 when he purchased 250 acres from the Dunham family. As early as 1816, Nashville newspapers ran notices advertising horses standing at stud at the Harding farm. In 1820, John built a brick, Federal-style home and named the entire property Belle Meade. By this time, he was becoming interested in racing his horses, and by 1823, he had registered his racing silks with the Nashville Jockey Club and was training horses on the track at his McSpadden's Bend farm, located across town.

Following his victory in 1881, Iroquois, the first American-bred horse to win the English Derby, retired to Belle Meade where he was treated as the family pet.

William Giles Harding, John's son, lived on the McSpadden's Bend property and worked with his father. By the time William Giles assumed management of the Belle Meade plantation, he was involved in several local jockey clubs and raced at all the area tracks including Clover Bottom, Gallatin, and Nashville.

In 1839 Harding brought a young enslaved boy to work at Belle Meade. His

Bob Green, 1900

name was Robert "Bob" Green. As he grew up working with the horses, he became Harding's right hand and was an expert in everything related to the Thoroughbred. Following the Civil War, Bob continued to work for the horse farm and, according to an 1879 ledger book in the Belle Meade archives, he was the highest paid worker on the farm as the head hostler or groom. The head groom at Belle Meade always wore a white apron, and Green was seen proudly wearing his apron even in New York City. In 1906, upon his death, he was granted his request for burial at the farm, where he rests today in an unmarked grave.

The Civil War interrupted horse breeding and racing in the South, but General Harding was able to keep all of his Thoroughbreds, even while other farms were having their horses requisitioned by both armies. After the war, he was able to continue his breeding program and, during 1867–1868, he won more purses than any living man in the United States. He was the first breeder in Tennessee to use the auction system for selling Thoroughbreds, and his Yearling sales, begun in 1867, were held annually until 1902. With the auction system, Belle Meade became the most successful Thoroughbred breeding farm the state would ever see. When General Harding died in 1886, *The Spirit of the Times* praised him as having done as much to promote horse breeding interests as any American in the nineteenth century.

In 1868, General William Hicks Jackson ("Billy") married General Harding's oldest daughter, Selene, and moved into the Belle Meade mansion. He, also, was an avid horseman and began working with his father-in-law to build up the breeding farm. By 1875, the decision was made to retire the racing silks and concentrate on breeding. After General Harding's death, Billy assumed one-third ownership of the horse farm with Selene's half-brother John, and Billy's brother Howell, who married Selene's sister, Mary Elizabeth. Billy's flair for entertaining and his confident, outgoing nature helped the farm to attract thousands of people to the yearling sales.

General Harding expanded the family home in 1853, creating the Greek Revival style seen today, and in 1883, Billy modernized the interior, adding wall-to-wall carpeting in all the downstairs rooms as well as three full bathrooms, complete with hot and cold running water. The family, due to its prominence in Nashville, hosted many dignitaries throughout the years, includ-

Upon the death of William Giles Harding, his son-in-law, former Confederate General William Hicks Jackson (1836-1903) of Paris, Tennessee, assumed management of Belle Meade and turned the plantation into one of America's most respected Thoroughbred breeding farms.

ing President and Mrs. Grover Cleveland, Robert Todd Lincoln, and Generals U.S. Grant, William T. Sherman, and Winfield Scott Hancock.

The list of Belle Meade's eminent horses reads like a "Who's Who" of American equine breeding. In 1842, the first famous stud at Belle Meade Plantation was Priam, named the American Thoroughbred Horse of the Year. After the Civil War, other outstanding horses at the plantation included Bonnie Scotland (1853–1880), acquired by William Giles Harding in 1872. Bonnie Scotland's descendants have persisted to modern times and include Northern Dancer, Never Say Die, Sunday Silence, and the 1973 Triple Crown winner, Secretariat. Iroquois was acquired by Billy Jackson in 1886 for $20,000 in gold. Iroquois became the first American-owned and -bred horse to win the English Derby in 1881. When the Americans learned of Iroquois' feat, they temporarily closed business on Wall Street to celebrate the victory. The same year, Iroquois also won the St. Ledger's Stakes and the Prince of Wales' Stakes and became the first horse, American or British, to win all three races in one year.

Enquirer (1867–1895) was named for the Cincinnati *Enquirer* newspaper and carried one of the best bloodlines. He was named best three-year-old of 1870. He is the only horse honored with a monument at Belle Meade. John R. McLean, publisher of the *Enquirer*, erected the monument during the Tennessee Centennial Exposition in 1897. Luke Blackburn (1877–1906), the son of Bonnie Scotland, became the longest-standing Belle Meade sire at twenty-two years. He sired Proctor Knott, Uncle Bob, and other winners and, in 1888, his descendants earned more than $100,000. Sadly, in 1904 the old champion sold for only $20 at the Belle Meade dispersal sale.

Dunham's Station, one of Nashville's early forts for protection against Indian attack, was the site that John Harding purchased in 1807 upon which to build Belle Meade.

Belle Meade is state headquarters for, and is administered by, the Association for the Preservation of Tennessee Antiquities (APTA).

BELMONT
DAVIDSON COUNTY
--- 1853 ---

When Adelicia Acklen's first husband died, he left her with an estate consisting of 750 slaves, seven cotton plantations in Louisiana, and a huge Middle Tennessee farm.

At one time, Nashville's Adelicia Hayes Franklin Acklen was described as the wealthiest woman in Tennessee and one of the richest in the United States. The Italianate mansion that she and her second husband, Joseph A. Acklen, built off the Hillsboro Road eventually grew to thirty-six rooms encompassing around ten thousand square feet of living space, with an additional 8,400 square feet of storage space in the basement. Ancillary buildings included a two-hundred-foot-long greenhouse, a tall brick water tower that is still visible today, a bowling alley, large carriage houses, stables, and a specially-built structure for the domesticated bears, all spread across the estate's nearly two hundred acres. A deer park and zoo added to the wonder of the magnificent home and gardens.

Adelicia's first husband was wealthy plantation owner Isaac Franklin. The highly successful Franklin had acquired numerous properties in Tennessee, Louisiana, and Texas. When he died in 1846, his estate, worth tens of millions of dollars by today's standards, passed to Adelicia, assuring her of a life free from financial problems.

Belmont was as widely known for its art, statuary, and fine furniture as its mistress was for the grand social events she hosted in the Grand Salon she had specially designed by eminent Nashville architect Adolphus Heiman. The vast gardens and grounds, designed with an Italian Renaissance flair, were impeccable, and offered a formal lawn, tea houses, and a veritable jungle of blooming shrubs and trees.

In 1867, four years after Joseph's untimely death, Adelicia married Dr. William Cheatham of Nashville in a wedding ceremony at Belmont that attracted nearly two thousand guests. In 1887, following the death of Dr. Cheatham, Belmont fell into the hands of others, including a development company, a school for young ladies, and finally, today's Belmont University. Adelicia died the same year in New York City. She is buried in Nashville's Mount Olivet Cemetery.

William Cooper portrait of Adelicia Acklen with her horse

Belmont is owned by Belmont University and administered by Belmont Mansion Association.

TRAVELLERS REST

⤙ 1799 ⤚

During the Battle of Nashville, in December 1864, Travellers Rest served as the command post for Confederate General John Bell Hood's Army of Tennessee, poised before the Union Army at Nashville.

In 1799, when John Overton built the first four rooms of his home upon an ancient Native American mound south of Nashville along the road to Franklin — a hall and parlor plan — the feat marked only the beginning of a building project that would go on for the next eighty-five years.

Before his long career was over, Overton, born in Louisa County, Virginia, in 1766, had served as an attorney, the supervisor of federal excise as a President George Washington appointee, judge on the Tennessee Superior Court of Law and Equity, Tennessee Supreme judge, co-founder of Memphis, and campaign manager for Andrew Jackson's presidential bid in 1824 and 1828. In the latter role, he often graciously hosted important politicos—Felix Grundy, John Henry Eaton, Sam Houston, and others—to the warmth of his library, housed in a separate building near the main house.

John Overton portrait by Ralph E. W. Earl

John Overton was not the first resident on the knoll upon which Travellers Rest was built. While digging out the cellar for his original house, Overton discovered many cultural artifacts and human bones that belonged to individuals of the Mississippian culture, who lived in Middle Tennessee and much of the South in the years between roughly 700 and 1500 AD. Of course, Overton knew nothing of these people, but in view of the many graves he discovered on his property, he aptly named his estate, "Golgotha" – hill of skulls.

The second phase of Travellers Rest occurred around 1811, when Overton added two rooms,

In 1828, John Overton added an ell, connecting the original structure with the kitchen.

one to each floor, giving the house, from the front approach, the early Federal style it has today. Overton also made use of beautiful woods in wainscoting the rooms of his house, and the meticulous design and arrangement of this lovely home bear out the fact that he was a man of good taste.

Overton married in 1820, late in life for the times. His bride was the daughter of General James White, the founder of Knoxville. In 1828, Overton added the expansive rear to the house. By then, the 2,300-acre estate was rising in

"The proudest moment of my life came when seven Confederate generals, in full battle dress, were seated at my dining table."

Harriet Maxwell Overton reminiscing about the days preceding the Battle of Nashville

prominence among Tennessee plantations, supported by at least fifty slaves who resided in quarters located north of the main house. Although cotton was the primary crop, Overton took an especial interest in raising fruit: grapes, pears, peaches, and pears, among others. The scion of Travellers Rest died at home in 1833, but his legacy was preserved by his son, Colonel John Overton, who continued to develop the property into one of the region's premier plantations.

A lover of formal gardens, Colonel Overton employed "a succession of foreign gardeners...an Irishman named Madden, Mr. Buchanan, a Scotchman who had worked as an under gardener in the famous Kew gardens in London, and Edward

Battle flag carried by the Army of Tennessee at the Battle of Nashville

Cross, an Englishman, who remained at Travellers Rest." The driveway from the main road to the manor house measured one-half mile, and it was lined with hardwood trees, roses, jasmine, and honeysuckle, as well as now long-forgotten flora such as crested moss, pink June, musk cluster, Texas rose, and giant of battle.

During the Civil War, Travellers Rest remained at the forefront of Nashville history. While the Battle of Nashville raged in December 1864, it served as the command post for Confederate General John Bell Hood's Army of Tennessee, poised before the Union Army at Nashville, following his embarrassing rout two weeks earlier at Franklin. During the second day of the battle, December 16, Hood's dreams of a renewed Confederacy were forever dashed among Overton's beloved fruit trees near the Peach Orchard.

Colonel Overton was not present with his family at Travellers Rest during the years of Federal occupation, as he was a fugitive from an arrest warrant issued by Secretary of War Stanton. In a bit of irony, fifty years after the war, Overton's son-in-law served in the same cabinet position – Secretary of War – in President Howard Taft's administration. Following the Battle of Nashville, Travellers Rest remained in the hands of Colonel Overton. After he died, the plantation stayed in the family and in 1929 was purchased by Jacob McGavock Dickinson, Jr.

General John Bell Hood, commander of Confederate forces at the Battle of Nashville, headquartered his command at Travellers Rest for two weeks in December 1864.

Since 1954, the Travellers Rest home and grounds have been held in public trust by the National Society of the Colonial Dames of America and are administered by the Travellers Rest Historic House Museum.

NATCHEZ TRACE

⟶ prehistory to early 19th century ⟵

*The Natchez Trace, linking the present-day cities of Nashville,
Tennessee, and Natchez, Mississippi, is among America's oldest roads.*

Established by great animal herds, especially bison, as they searched for salt
licks in the vast eastern forests, the Natchez Trace later provided a
communications link for both prehistoric and historic groups of Indians plying
trade among themselves throughout the southeastern United States. Thus, the
thoroughfare was already ancient when Anglo pioneers first utilized the route.

After present-day Middle Tennessee and Central Kentucky had been settled by
Virginians and North Carolinians during the mid-to-late 1770s, the region was
gradually turned into small farmsteads that were used primarily to feed the owner
and his family. In time, however, surpluses of foodstuffs occurred and farmers sought
markets for the excess produce. The principal marketplaces were Natchez and New
Orleans and the fastest method for reaching them was to place the produce onboard
flatboats and to float downstream along the Cumberland and Kentucky Rivers to the
Ohio. From there, the farmer and his boat floated down the Ohio to the Mississippi.

The task of getting the produce to the markets, while entailing hard work, was
fairly simple. The real problem occurred after the farmer sold his goods and attempted
to return home. Steamboats did not exist at the time, leaving only two options: using
the river system, a nearly impossible task when considering the entire trip would be
upstream, or walking back home through the wilderness.

The 450-mile-long Natchez Trace provided the farmer with
the overland means of travel, either on foot or horseback,
which returned him to Nashville. Although more
convenient and less difficult than the water route upriver,
the Trace option still had its problems. As soon as
numbers of northward-bound farmers increased, carrying
considerable amounts of cash from the sale of their
commodities, highwaymen intent on relieving them of
their newfound wealth proliferated along the route.

Captain Meriwether
Lewis, 1807, by
Charles Willson Peale,
painted the year
following the return
of Lewis and Clark
from their expedition
to the Pacific Ocean
and two years prior to
Lewis's death on the
Natchez Trace

Opposite: Segment of
the original Trace in
Maury County

Meriwether Lewis's
tomb at Grinder's
Stand where he died.

Before long, a trip along the Natchez Trace proved to be a dangerous adventure and many unfortunate travelers were robbed and murdered along the way.

Following the successful arrival of the first steamboat at New Orleans in 1811, the popularity of the Natchez Trace waned for farmers traveling back and forth between Tennessee and Kentucky in the north and Natchez and New Orleans in the south. However, by then, mail service between Nashville and Natchez had been established and the United States Army had been utilized to improve the road and to make it more accessible and safer to the everyday traveler.

Bridge at Brown's
Creek in Williamson
County

Following the War of 1812, the federal government deemed that its national road system needed vast improvements to meet the communications and transportation requirements of the growing country. In 1817, the first major project, "General Jackson's Military Road," connected Columbia, Tennessee, just south of Nashville, with Madisonville, Louisiana, across Lake Pontchartrain from New Orleans. Compared to the Natchez Trace, the new road provided much improved and advanced travel, and the old Trace gradually fell into disrepair. During its time of popularity, not only did the Natchez Trace carry northward-bound farmers back home

The house of ferry operator John Gordon, who, in the early 1800s, made an agreement with the Chickasaw chief to operate a trading post and ferry on the nearby Duck River. Military expeditions with General Andrew Jackson kept Gordon away from home much of the time and his wife, Dorathea, supervised much of the construction in 1817-18.

to Tennessee and Kentucky, but it also transported thousands of emigrants southward to lower Mississippi, Louisiana, and eventually Texas. Its role in the nation's westward expansion is undeniable.

The sights and sounds of the old Natchez Trace can once again be savored along its modern-day counterpart, the Natchez Trace Parkway. Dedicated in May 1938 as an official unit of the National Park system, the parkway today is one of the most visited units within the system. Many historic sites still exist along the Tennessee portion of the Trace, much unchanged from the time when "Kaintucks" plodded their way back home from New Orleans and Natchez. One such site, the Gordon House, is located at the Trace's crossing of the Duck River. The two-story brick home was built during 1818 and 1819 by the wife of Virginia-born Indian fighter, ferry operator, and first Nashville postmaster, John Gordon, during his absence fighting the Seminole Indians in Florida. John Gordon died in 1819, having enjoyed his new home less than one year.

A few miles south of the Gordon House is the stone monument erected in 1848 by the State of Tennessee to the memory of Captain Meriwether Lewis, co-commander of the famed Lewis and Clark Expedition to the Pacific Ocean and back during 1804–1806. Lewis died nearby while journeying from St. Louis to Washington D.C. on official business. The existing log house is not original, but it does reside near the site of Grinder's Stand, where Lewis died on October 11, 1809.

Next spread: Coursing the crest of the Highland Rim in Middle Tennessee, the Natchez Trace has afforded travelers from early times to present, views of the verdant Duck River Valley.

The Natchez Trace Parkway is a unit of the U.S. National Park Service.

HIRAM MASONIC HALL

WILLIAMSON COUNTY

↦ 1823 ↤

Hiram Masonic Hall is the oldest Gothic Revival building in Tennessee and one of the oldest in the nation.

Although Masons have met regularly in Franklin since 1809, when Hiram Lodge No. 7 was organized, the first public record of the group dates to July 1812, when the county court allowed them to gather at the courthouse. They had no permanent home in town until 1823 when the Masonic Hall on Cameron Street (present-day Second Avenue) was completed, which was, at the time, the tallest, and only, three-story building in Tennessee. The hall is a grandiose Gothic Revival building, an early example in the United States of that architectural style. In addition to providing meeting facilities for the Masons, the lodge has also opened its doors to many fledgling churches in the area, allowing their congregations to freely gather until permanent space could be acquired. St. Paul's Episcopal Church was organized there in 1827, and members of the Church of Christ and the Presbyterian Church have also assembled in the lodge.

Franklin and the surrounding region provided the nation with many influential men during the period from 1820 to 1850, among them Andrew Jackson, James K. Polk, Thomas Hart Benton, James Robertson, John Bell, Felix Grundy, and John Eaton. All of these men, and others, have attended affairs at the Masonic Hall, either as Masons, church-goers, or guests at political affairs. One of the liveliest dealings must surely have been in August 1830, when President Andrew Jackson and his secretary-of-war, Franklin native John Eaton, met with a delegation of Chickasaw Indians during the administration's early phases of Indian Removal. For several days local residents watched in awe as the colorfully attired Chickasaws wandered sadly around Franklin, while their chiefs negotiated for the tribe's removal west of the Mississippi River. Ironically, the entire proceedings were for naught since the United States Senate never ratified the treaty and it had to be renegotiated two years later.

This rare York Rite apron, which belonged to a Franklin Mason of the 1820s, is made of lambskin and embroidered with the seal of Solomon, representing the building of King Solomon's Temple by stonemasons.

Hiram Mason Hall continues as an active lodge for Hiram Lodge No. 7.

CARNTON PLANTATION

⟶ 1826 ⟵

On November 30, 1864, Carnton Plantation, located south of Franklin off Lewisburg Pike, witnessed one of the most calamitous and horribly terrific battles in American history. Its role in that event and the aftermath would link Carnton forever, and inextricably, to the legacy of the Civil War.

Randal McGavock (1768–1843), builder of Carnton, emigrated from Virginia in 1796 and settled in Nashville. He was involved in local and state politics and eventually served as mayor of Nashville from 1824 to 1825. The following year, McGavock moved his family to the recently completed Carnton, named after his father's birthplace in County Antrim, Ireland.

After the senior McGavock's death in 1843, his son John inherited the plantation. The McGavocks grew wheat, corn, oats, hay, and potatoes, in addition to raising thoroughbred horses. In December 1848, John McGavock married his cousin, Carrie Winder, of Ducros Plantation in Louisiana, and they had five children during the subsequent years, three of whom died at a young age.

In 1847 John McGavock added a two-story Greek Revival portico and two dormers in the attic. A few years later, the couple added a two-story porch onto the rear of the house, which extended at one end to take advantage of southerly breezes. The interior was also updated in the 1850s, with the addition of fashionable wallpapers, carpets, and paint. The central passage currently appears much as it was during the Civil War years, with restored paint colors and an original wallpaper pattern reproduced from a fragment that remains in place at the top of the stairs. The parlor was upgraded by adding a Greek Revival mantel, new wallpaper, and wall-to-wall carpeting.

Carnton grew to become one of the premier farms in Williamson County, Tennessee. The Federal-style

Carrie Winder, daughter of a Louisiana plantation owner, married John McGavock, her cousin, in 1848 and became the mistress of one of Tennessee's foremost plantations.

Today, the Confederate Cemetery is a somber reminder of the terrible carnage that occurred at Franklin on the evening of November 30, 1864.

plantation house became a social and political center where McGavock entertained Andrew Jackson and James K. Polk and presided over an estate that eventually grew to 1,420 acres.

Beginning at 4 p.m. on November 30, 1864, Carnton was witness to one of the bloodiest battles of the entire Civil War. Everything the McGavock family ever knew was forever changed. The Confederate Army of Tennessee furiously assaulted the Federal army entrenched along the southern edge of Franklin. The

"The wounded, in hundreds, were brought to [the house] during the battle, and all the night after. And when the noble old house could hold no more, the yard was appropriated until the wounded and dead filled that."

Confederate Staff Officer

resulting battle, believed to be the bloodiest five hours of the Civil War, involved a massive frontal assault larger than Pickett's Charge at Gettysburg. The majority of the combat occurred in the dark and at close quarters. The Battle of Franklin lasted barely five hours and led to some 9,500 soldiers being killed, wounded, captured, or counted as missing. Nearly 7,000 of that number were Confederate troops.

Following the battle, Carnton served as the largest field hospital in the area for

Franklin's Confederate Cemetery was made possible by John and Carrie McGavock, who donated the site from land that was part of their own family burial plot. This photograph was taken in 1869.

hundreds of wounded and dying Confederate soldiers. The McGavocks and their two children, Hattie (age nine) and Winder (age seven), assisted the surgeons and tended to the needs of the wounded. Several hundred eventually came to Carnton and 150 died during the first night. Bloodstains are still visible in several rooms. They are heaviest in the children's bedroom, which was used as an operating room. The floors of the restored home are still stained with the blood of the men who were treated there.

Upon her death in 1905, Carrie Winder McGavock was eulogized by *The New York Times* as the "Widow of the South."

On the morning of December 1, 1864, the bodies of four Confederate generals killed during the fighting—Patrick R. Cleburne, Hiram B. Granbury, John Adams, and Otho F. Strahl—lay on Carnton's back porch awaiting removal to their final resting places. Most of the over 1,750 Confederate dead were buried on the battlefield, their graves marked by wooden headboards inscribed with the soldier's name, company, and regiment. Over the months, the writing faded, and the markers began to disappear.

In early 1866, John and Carrie McGavock designated two acres of land adjacent to their family cemetery as a final burial place for nearly 1,500 Confederate soldiers killed during the battle. The McGavocks maintained the cemetery until their respective deaths. Today, the McGavock Confederate Cemetery is a lasting memorial honoring those fallen soldiers and the Battle of Franklin. It is the largest privately owned military cemetery in the nation.

Carnton Plantation is under the stewardship of the Battle of Franklin Trust.

CARTER HOUSE
ⵚ 1830 ⵚ

Within five hours, the Battle of Franklin was history, and nearly ten thousand soldiers, representing both sides of the conflict, lay dead or wounded upon the killing fields surrounding the Carter House.

At a few minutes past 3:00 p.m. on November 30, 1864, the Kentucky, Indiana, Ohio, and Illinois farm boys who made up the majority of General John M. Schofield's Union army at Franklin, peered southward over the massive breastworks they had just completed only hours earlier and beheld a sight few of them had ever witnessed before. Streaming toward them, along Columbia Pike through the gap between Winstead and Breezy Hills, more than one hundred regiments of Confederate infantry troops, augmented by artillery and cavalry units, burst forth upon the farmland and pastures leading toward Franklin. Regimental bands alternated playing "Dixie," "The Girl I Left Behind," and "Bonnie Blue Flag," while divisional banners and guidons waved in the wind. A few minutes later, Lieutenant Edwin H. Rennolds of the 5th Tennessee Regiment (CSA) exclaimed, "It was the grandest sight I ever beheld," as he watched thousands of his fellow foot soldiers pour northward across the open ground that lay between Winstead Hill and the Union breastworks near the Carter House to attack the soldiers of Union General George D. Wagner.

While history was being made on the plains south of Franklin, an equally dramatic and moving scene involving one of the town's native sons was being played out nearby at the Carter House, the focus of the bloody battle. While the chaotic sounds of the raging battle echoed above the Carter family, holed up in the basement of the farm house for protection, their youngest son, Tod, was leading in the forefront of the Confederate assault. Spurring his horse forward over his family farm, Carter shouted, "Follow me boys, I am almost home!"

Tod Carter, photographed just before leaving for the war

153

South-facing wall of the Carter farm office, which was at the center of the Federal breastworks, and bears the scars of the Confederate attack.

Tod Carter's spurs.

When young Theodorick (Tod) Carter left his home on the outskirts of Franklin in 1861 to fight in the Civil War, he could not have realized that the next time he would see his family would be from his deathbed. Marching off to a hero's departure, Tod believed, like most other Southerners, that the ensuing conflict would be a short-lived one and that he would be back home with his family in no time at all.

During the previous three years, Carter had fought valiantly in several campaigns with the Army of Tennessee under a number of commanders. Never once in that period had he been furloughed home to see his family. As a captain in General John Bell Hood's advancing army, he now anxiously looked upon his beloved village, not as the innocent youngster who had left in a shower of hurrahs and band music but as a seasoned veteran who wanted nothing more than for the awful bloodletting to be over.

Late in the evening of November 30, as the noise of small arms fire subsided, a messenger rode up and knocked on the door of the Carter home and informed Tod's frightened relatives that their kinsman had been severely wounded just a few feet away in his own backyard. The battered youth was carefully delivered to his parents' waiting arms. Eight-year-old Alice McPhail Nichol, who lived with the Carter family, remembered that Tod had been found "lying face down thrown over his horse's head." He had been shot nine times in both arms, both legs, and in the

"Bullets rained against the house, and a cannon ball went crashing through."

Moscow Carter

head. Two days later, finally at home after being separated from his family for so long, Tod Carter died in the bed in which he was born and was laid to rest about a mile north of his homeplace, in Franklin's Rest Haven Cemetery.

The scene at the Carter House the morning following the battle was inconceivable. The intense hand-to-hand fighting had exacted horrific carnage. Five-star general Douglas MacArthur's then nineteen-year-old father, Arthur, was severely wounded, but survived. The bravery exhibited the previous evening resulted in the awarding of thirteen Congressional Medals of Honor for valor.

Military buckles recovered from the Carter Farm following the battle

The home was built between 1828 and 1830 by Fountain Branch Carter, the father of Tod and Moscow, who had migrated to Williamson County from Virginia in 1806. The house's sizeable rooms, high ceilings, and imposing staircase all combine to give the impression of a much larger unit. The plan of the house is typically Middle Tennessee, with a parlor located on either side of the entrance hall. The stairs lead into a small hall above and two bedrooms with low ceilings. A one-story ell runs from behind the right-hand parlor and contains two additional rooms, one of which is the dining room. The kitchen, traditionally detached from the main house, is in the backyard, within easy walking distance of the dining room. The two side rooms, as well as the downstairs bedroom and the entrance hall, all have outside doors leading to a one-story back porch.

Chair railings in the downstairs rooms and hall and a tasteful blend of wallpapers and paint lend a quiet beauty to the Carter House. These features, combined with the original hardwood floors, give a feeling of the gracious lifestyle existing here when the Carter family was in residence. An office, tool shed, and smokehouse complete the dependencies on the Carter grounds, all of which, even today, display the effects of pounding small arms and artillery fire. The farm office stands as the most heavily damaged building from the Civil War still in existence.

View of the Carter House, farm office, kitchen, and family garden - c. 1895

The Carter House is owned by the State of Tennessee and administered by the Tennessee Historical Commission through the Battle of Franklin Trust.

HOMESTEAD MANOR

—◆ *1819* ◆—

*The bravery of a teenaged girl wins the day for an embattled
Confederate army.*

When Francis Giddens and his wife and family moved to Williamson County
in 1800, he was determined to build a home in the grand tradition to which he was
accustomed back in Virginia. Settling on a Revolutionary War land grant near
present-day Thompson Station, Giddens and his son eventually acquired hundreds
of acres of additional prime real estate along Murfree's Fork before beginning
construction on the home. In the meantime, the family lived in a small log cabin
during the land acquisition period and the ten years it took to physically complete

the manor house, but, finally, in 1819, it was ready to be occupied.

Homestead Manor was built of hand-made bricks, meticulously crafted and laid by the Giddens' slaves. Even the interior walls are brick, extending from the foundation all the way up to the third floor. A two-story porch, supported by six round columns, provides an imposing entrance to the house. Added at a later date, the porch gives a Greek Revival aspect to the basically Georgian-style architecture of the home.

Large double parlors, a dining room, and a large kitchen with both a fireplace and a back staircase, dominate the first floor. A central hallway measuring thirty-seven feet deep divides the house equally into right and left portions. Twelve-foot ceilings are universal throughout the building, and original mantel pieces dominate the nine fireplaces. The second floor, reached by a straight flight staircase, is divided by a similar center hallway. The third floor, again with the deep center hallway, consists of two huge rooms.

During the final stages of his home's construction in 1819, Giddens decided that his property would provide a perfect location for an ordinary, or hostelry, wherein stagecoach passengers and other travelers making the trip between

Alice Thompson, the
young Confederate
heroine

Franklin and Columbia and points beyond, could get a couple of good meals and a pleasant night's rest. He applied to the Williamson County court for a permit to operate such an establishment in the building.

During the Battle of Thompson Station on March 5, 1863, Homestead Manor—since inherited by Giddens' daughter, Nancy Word, but owned at the time by the Thomas Banks family—was in the midst of the heated action. Violent fighting between the Confederate forces of Generals Earl Van Dorn and Nathan Bedford Forrest, and Union commander Colonel John Coburn, occurred on a hill north of the house. A cellar room in the southwest corner of the building was used as a place of refuge by the family and a few neighbors during the spirited battle. One of these neighbors was a seventeen-year-old girl named Alice Thompson, the daughter of Dr. Elijah Thompson, for whom the village of Thompson Station was named.

"At this site, General Earl Van Dorn's Confederate Cavalry Corps defeated a Federal task force under Col. John Colburn; he along with 1220 officers and men were captured. The outcome was decided by Forrest's Brigade which overran the Federal left several hundred yards northeast in a flank attack."

Tennessee Historical Marker, U. S. Highway 31 at Thompson Station Road

As the fighting moved frighteningly close to Homestead Manor, Alice, observing that one of the Confederate color-bearers had been wounded, rushed from her place of safety, scooped up the flag, and encouraged the faltering Southerners to forge forward. It is reported that Colonel S. G. Earle, the commander of the Arkansas regiment surrounding the house, screamed to his men, "Boys, a woman has your flag!" Hustling Miss Thompson back to safety, the regiment pursued the Union forces and assisted in winning the day for the Confederacy. Afterward, Homestead Manor was used as a temporary field hospital to treat the nearly four hundred Confederate casualties.

In time, Homestead Manor passed into the ownership of Dr. and Mrs. William Darby, who maintained it for years. Upon their deaths, the property was acquired by Mr. and Mrs. Jay Franks.

The colors carried by the Arkansas regiment and rescued by Alice Thompson was a "Van Dorn Flag" similar to this battle scarred flag.

Homestead Manor is operated as Homestead Manor
Plantation Restaurant and Tea Room by Jay and
Marcia Franks.

JAMES K. POLK HOME

MAURY COUNTY

⟶ c. 1816 ⟶

This house in Columbia was the home of young James K. Polk, who matured to become a congressman, the speaker of the U.S. House of Representatives, and governor of Tennessee, before being elected to the office of eleventh president of the United States.

While North Carolina-born James K. Polk (1795–1849) was attending college in his native state, his father and mother, Samuel and Jane Knox Polk, began construction of this house in Columbia, Tennessee. Young Polk, the oldest of ten children, and his family had moved to Middle Tennessee around 1806 and settled in the region where several members of the extended Polk family had already set down roots. James K. Polk would call this property—and much later, Polk Place in Nashville—his permanent homes throughout his political service to Tennessee and the United States.

Samuel Polk erected his modest, Federal-style home on one of Columbia's main streets. Next door, in 1820, he also built another home, called "the Sisters' House," wherein two of James K. Polk's married sisters lived from time to time. Situated on a corner lot, the property also contains the reconstructed kitchen, courtyard, and formal gardens.

Early in his political career, Polk had embraced the tenets of "Jacksonian Democracy," even earning the sobriquet "Young Hickory," and looked toward his friend and protégé Andrew Jackson as a mentor for his own political philosophies and aspirations. Polk studied law under the noted Judge Felix Grundy, who throughout his long career served as a congressman, U.S. senator, and U.S. attorney-general in President Martin Van Buren's administration.

In 1823, James Knox Polk was elected to the Tennessee House of Representatives from Maury County. At the time the state legislature met at Murfreesboro, and it was during this period of Polk's life that he met his future wife, Sarah Childress, who lived in the capital city. The couple married in

Cameo worn by Sarah Polk was made by New York artist Salathiel Ellis and features a miniature of President Polk attributed to the painter Debousier.

HAMILTON PLACE

~ *1832* ~

Hamilton Place is one of four distinctive homes along the
Columbia-Mt. Pleasant Highway built and occupied by the sons of
Colonel William Polk.

During the early part of the nineteenth century, North Carolina native
William Polk (1758–1834) was one of the largest landowners in Tennessee and
may have controlled as much as 100,000 acres of rich Middle Tennessee real
estate. During the Revolution, after being shot in the mouth, he earned the
sobriquet of the officer "who caught British bullets in his teeth." The veteran

served at Germantown and Valley Forge with General George Washington, who, later, as president of the United States, appointed him to the position of supervisor of Internal Revenue for the District of North Carolina. Although a large part of Polk's private domain was acquired through speculation, one tract containing nearly six thousand acres in Maury County was obtained when he supposedly won it during a game of whit or "rattle and snap" with the governor of North Carolina, hence the property's name. Polk eventually subdivided the Rattle and Snap property, giving a portion to each of his four sons—Lucius J., Leonidas, George W., and Rufus K. In this manner, Lucius J. acquired the land upon which Hamilton Place, located on the Columbia-Mt. Pleasant highway, was built in 1832.

Once upon a time during a visit to Andrew Jackson's Hermitage, Lucius had met a young woman named Mary Jane Eastin, the great-niece of Rachel Jackson. The two young people's paths may have crossed again from time to time and, although Lucius thought of Mary Jane often, he did little to woo her. That is, until one day when news reached Maury County that she was to wed a naval officer

PINSON MOUNDS
MADISON COUNTY
⭈ c. *1500 AD* ⭈

The Pinson Mounds, located in Madison County a few miles from Jackson, were first explored by white residents soon after the Chickasaw tribe ceded present-day West Tennessee to the United States in 1818.

Tennessee abounds in the material culture left by several groups of prehistoric native inhabitants, including those of the period known as Woodland. Woodland people lived in small villages, practiced a simple form of agriculture, made and used pottery, and hunted game with bows and arrows. They also constructed mounds,

hence their once-popular name, "Mound Builders." The Woodland period followed the Archaic culture, whose people were hunter-gatherers, and preceded the Mississippian period in which large towns, replete with massive ceremonial mounds were constructed.

Land speculator, Joel Pinson, was the first to see the wonders of the Pinson site, a 400-acre complex located on a broad plain along the Forked Deer River and containing at least thirty mounds with heights attaining as much as 72 feet. J. G. Cisco, a Jackson newspaperman, popularized the mounds during the late 1800s. In 1916, Smithsonian Institution archaeologist William Edward Myer arrived on the site and performed an elaborate survey. Since then the site has been studied numerous times by Tennessee Division of Archaeology scientists who have determined that artifacts discovered there prove that the Pinson community was part of a large-scale trading complex linking prehistoric sites throughout the eastern United States.

Saul's Mound, the tallest in the Pinson site, rises seventy-two feet above the plain of the Forked Deer River.

Skull rattles unearthed at Pinson were created from human skulls and engraved with ceremonial designs.

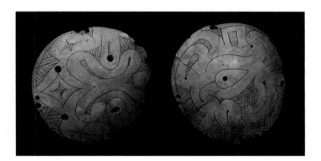

The Pinson Mounds complex is managed by the Tennessee Department of Environment and Conservation, State Parks Division.

173

TEMPLE ADAS ISRAEL

→ 1881–1882 →

The Jewish congregation that has convened at Brownsville, Tennessee, since the 1860s has never had a full-time rabbi and its leadership has been filled by a number of lay readers, including Emil Tamm, Abe Sternberger, Morton Felsenthal, Fred Silverstein, and Fred Silverstein, Jr.

The first Jewish settler to arrive in North America was Jacob Barsimson, who stepped ashore on Manhattan Island on July 8, 1654, despite the protests of New Amsterdam (present-day New York) Governor Peter Stuyvesant. Since that long-ago day, Jewish immigrants by the boatloads have risked life and limb to migrate to the United States, among them German-born Joseph Sternberger, who eventually moved to Brownsville, Tennessee, during the 1860s, bringing with him an ancient copy of the *Torah*. Soon afterward, Jacob and Karoline Felsenthal became Sternberger's friends, and, within a few years, the threesome organized the Adas Israel congregation which for several years met at the homes of local Jews, including the Anker and Rothschild families.

Temple Adas, a two-hundred-seat synagogue, was built at the corner of Washington and College Streets in Brownsville and dedicated in 1882. At the ceremonies, Emil Tamm gave a speech in which he thanked his Christian neighbors for the financial support they had given to the erection of the synagogue. "The new temple was filled to overflowing with Jewish members…and a host of non-Jewish worshipers of every religious denomination in the city," wrote a journalist for the local newspaper.

The building's design was based on that of the United Hebrew Congregation Temple in Louisville, Kentucky, and is an example of religious Gothic Revival architecture. A set of thirteen Gothic-style, stained glass windows was installed in 1910. An unusual feature of the original building was a steeple, which was removed during a renovation in the 1920s. The original wooden siding was also replaced by brick at that time and an organ and new pews were added.

The stained glass window above the Torah ark is unusual in a synagogue in that it depicts a large, realistic human eye, similar to the Eye of Providence found on the one-dollar bill and in Masonic iconography.

The temple exterior was originally wood clapboard and featured a steeple, also unusual for a synagogue.

Temple Adas Israel is an active synagogue.

LA GRANGE

FAYETTE COUNTY

-◦- *incorporated in 1831* -◦-

For nearly two centuries, evening summer breezes from nearby Mississippi have blown across the wide plains of moonlit cotton fields and up the gentle hills, cooling the gracious verandas and columned porches of La Belle Village.

La Grange is an iconic monument to the antebellum era of the Old South. During the 1830s, while Memphis was still a rough and rowdy river town, La Grange was establishing itself as a sophisticated center of commerce, education, and gracious society as the population soared to over 3,000. Educational academies, several businesses, hotels, and three newspapers were established. In 1835 La Grange stockholders chartered the La Grange & Memphis Railway, the first railroad in the state of Tennessee and the second in the entire South. The La Grange Female College, founded in 1854, instructed ladies from all over the South in music, languages, and other academic disciplines.

Stock certificate for the La Grange and Memphis Railroad, the first railroad chartered in Tennessee

Opposite: Woodlawn Plantation - the 1828 home of War of 1812 veteran Major Charles Michie and the Western Tennessee headquarters for General William T. Sherman during the 1862 Federal occupation of La Grange

Serenity, c. 1858, was, like many homes in the town, used as a hospital during the Civil War.

Woodlawn Plantation was built in 1828 by a War of 1812 veteran, Major Charles Michie, upon land deeded to him for his military service. The Greek Revival-style home was used as the western Tennessee headquarters for General William T. Sherman during the area's occupation in 1862 by the Union army. Woodlawn, as well as many other homes in La Grange, was used as a field hospital during the conflict. As a consequence of the town being strategically positioned along the railroad, many Union troops were quartered there, augmented by a large portion of General Ulysses S. Grant's retreating soldiers from Grant's first attempt to occupy Vicksburg, Mississippi, during late 1862.

It was from La Grange that Union Major Benjamin Henry Grierson launched the famous "Grierson's Raid" deep into Mississippi during late April and early May 1863. Cutting communications links and destroying railroads along the way, Grierson's bold maneuvers proved critical to General Grant's second attempt to occupy Vicksburg, by drawing away Confederate units to pursue him and minimize the havoc he was causing. On May 2, Grierson and his command arrived at Baton Rouge, Louisiana, after having "taken the heart out of Mississippi," according to Grant.

The Allen Cogbill Home, c. 1847, is shaded by a large, state champion water oak tree.

Other magnificent antebellum homes in La Grange include the Allan Cogbill home (1847), a Greek Revival style which suffered heavy damage in the 1900 tornado, causing the two present-day balconies to represent different styles. Hancock Hall (1857) was built by Dr. J. J. Pulliam, who enjoyed his home for only a brief time before it was occupied by Union troops. General Grant is reputed to have experienced a lovely dinner there. On occasion, Grant's wife would visit, and could be observed taking pleasurable horseback rides through the village. Likewise, many of the other fine homes in the village were commandeered for a brief time by Federal officers as the Union army continued its occupation of southwest Tennessee.

La Grange is enmeshed within a forest of several hundred magnolia trees, heightening the town's Deep South atmosphere.

The village of La Grange is a collection of private residences open on special occasion tour weekends.

HUNT-PHELAN HOUSE

—*first stage-1830*—
—*second stage-1855*—

During most of the Civil War, the Hunt-Phelan House served a number of military functions, including being used as the headquarters for General Ulysses S. Grant in planning the siege of Vicksburg, followed by a two-year stint as a Union hospital.

The Hunt-Phelan House, located on historic Beale Street, dates back to the very early years of Memphis. It was designed by Robert Mills, who also drew the plans for the Washington Monument in the nation's capital. George H. Wyatt built the first part of the house in 1830. The red-brick, Federal-style structure contained sixteen rooms and an escape tunnel that was used during the Civil War and later by the Underground Railroad. When Wyatt was bitten by the California "gold bug" in 1849, he sold the house to Jesse Tate, who, in 1850, sold it to Eli and Julia Driver. Around 1855, the Driver family added a two-story ell to be used for servants' quarters and a kitchen. The original front portico was moved to the side and a new two-story portico with Ionic columns was added to the front, giving the house a Greek Revival look.

A son-in-law of the Drivers, William Harding Hunt, inherited the home shortly before the Civil War. During the summer of 1862, as General Ulysses S. Grant and Union commanders planned the attack on Vicksburg, Mississippi, the structure was a hubbub of activity as generals pored over maps and issued orders to their subordinates. Shortly after Grant's departure, the home became the headquarters for the Western Sanitary Commission that provided housing for Freedman's Bureau teachers, as well as for soldiers. In 1865, control of the property was returned to Hunt by President Andrew Johnson.

Stephen Rice Phelan, a former geologist for Standard Oil Company, acquired the house early in the twentieth century. In years past, it was visited by a string of notables, including presidents Andrew Jackson, Martin Van Buren, Andrew Johnson, and Grover Cleveland, in addition to CSA president Jefferson Davis and southern generals Leonidas Polk and Nathan Bedford Forrest.

General Ulysses S. Grant planned the siege of Vicksburg in the dining room of the Hunt mansion.

The Hunt-Phelan operates as an inn and fine dining restaurant.

189

VICTORIAN VILLAGE
HISTORIC DISTRICT
⊷ mid- to late 1800s ⊶

A grand collection of Victorian mansions situated on or around Adams Avenue near downtown Memphis is a reflection of wealth and glamour of the Golden Age of steamboats and agricultural commerce.

The Victorian Village Historic District extends from 198 to 680 Adams Avenue, once known as "Millionaires Row," near downtown Memphis. In this compact neighborhood, several houses have been preserved from the Victorian era, most of them displaying a multitude of nuances and design elements used by American architects during the period from the early 1840s until the early 1900s. One of these structures, the Mallory-Neely House, is a superb example of Victorian architectural style and its variations.

The Mallory-Neely House, located at 652 Adams Avenue, was built in 1852 in the Italian Villa style. The home's first owner, Isaac Kirkland, a local banker, lived there until 1864, when he sold it to Benjamin Babb, a Memphis cotton factor. Babb sold it in 1883 to another cotton factor, James Columbus Neely, who moved in with his wife, Frances, and their five children. In 1900, one of Neely's daughters, Daisy, married yet another cotton factor named Barton Lee Mallory and the couple raised three children in the home.

The house has undergone several renovations over the years. During the late nineteenth century, the Neelys added one-half story, making the structure a three-story affair and creating a twenty-five room, 16,000-square-foot abode, while at the same time enlarging the central tower. High Victorian elements were represented throughout the interior, including such features as *faux* grained woodwork, parquet flooring, ceiling stenciling, and carved mantelpieces. Stained glass windows, purchased during a visit to the 1893 Columbian Exposition in Chicago, and rare

Gate to Mallory-Neely House

Opposite: Mallory-Neely House - 1852, originally the home of cotton factor Benjamin Babb, the house was purchased in 1883 by another cotton factor, James Columbus Neely. In 1900 the house became the residence of his youngest daughter, Daisy Neely Mallory, until her death in 1969 at age ninety-eight.

Oriental décor from the Louisiana Purchase Exposition in St. Louis a decade later, added to the charm of the library, dining room, and entrance hall.

Mrs. Mallory passed away in 1938, her husband thirty-one years later. In 1972, the Neely family deeded the site to the Daughters, Sons, and Children of the American Revolution. Fifteen years later, the house and surrounding property were acquired by the Memphis Park Commission and Memphis Museums, Inc.

Other outstanding properties along Adams Avenue are equally as impressive as the Mallory-Neely House. The Woodruff-Fontaine House, at 680 Adams, a French Victorian mansion, was built in 1870 by Amos Woodruff following the designs of two premier Memphis architects, Edward C. Jones and Matthias Harvey Baldwin. In 1883, Noland Fontaine, the president of the world's third-largest cotton company at the time, purchased the home. The city of Memphis acquired the property in 1936 and for several years, the house remained vacant, the victim of advancing deterioration. In 1962, the Association for the Preservation of Tennessee Antiquities (APTA) obtained the home and restored it.

The Harsson-Goyer-Lee House, the Pillow-McIntyre House, and the Massey

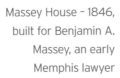

Harsson-Goyer-Lee House – c. 1843-1871, was once the home of riverboat owner James Lee.

Massey House – 1846, built for Benjamin A. Massey, an early Memphis lawyer

Woodruff-Fontaine House - 1871, built by Amos Woodruff, carriage manufacturer and president of two banks. Amos's daughter Mollie was married to Egbert Woolridge in the house and they resided in a second-floor suite. Within four years her infant son and husband died from illnesses only months apart in the same bedroom. Reportedly, the ghosts of Mollie, her husband, and child continue to haunt the mansion.

House, as well as several other structures, complement the Victorian Village Historic District. The Magevney House at 198 Adams Avenue is neither Victorian in design, nor a mansion, but rather a small, clapboard cottage similar, no doubt, to many other homes built during this early period of Memphis history. One of the oldest remaining residences in Memphis, the home was built during the 1830s and was the site of the first Catholic mass, wedding, and baptism in Memphis. The City of Memphis acquired the property in 1941.

"Victorianism refers to the reign of Queen Victoria of England (1837–1901). The design of this period might be characterized as dynamic, innovative and a general trend away from Classicism. It was a period of technological innovation in building and changes of style, as the consequence of aesthetic and philosophical controversy. Designs were derived mainly from the Baroque and Gothic styles."

The Camron-Stanford House Preservation Association, 2003

Pillow-McIntyre House - 1852, purchased in 1873 by Mexican War and Confederate General Gideon Pillow.

Chucalissa Site
⤙ *1400–1500 AD* ⤚

"The site is known for its excellent preservation of architectural, floral, faunal, and human osteological materials."

Statement of Significance, National Historic Landmarks Program, 1994

During the years immediately preceding Hernando De Soto's *entrada* into the southeastern part of the present-day United States in 1539, natives belonging to the Mississippian culture populated the entire region. Large towns, massive temple mounds, the practice of agriculture, an extensive trade network, and a high degree of artistic ability were hallmarks of this lifestyle. One of the culture's best-preserved

The Chucalissa Site is administered by the Memphis University Archeology Science Department.

and illustrative sites in the entire Mississippi River valley is Chucalissa. Originally situated upon a bluff above the east bank of the Mississippi, it now lies a few miles inland above an ox-bow lake left from a bend of the river after it changed its course.

When the Mississippian culture mysteriously disappeared in the early sixteenth century, the vacuum created by its exit was filled by several historic tribes of Indians, including, in the southwestern Tennessee region, the Chickasaws. However, the name, "Chucalissa," is a modern Choctaw word meaning "house abandoned."

Early archaeological excavations at Chucalissa were performed under the auspices of the Tennessee Division of State Parks and yielded significant artifacts, including earthenware utensils created with artistic effigy images. The excavation often involved assistance from inmates at the local penal farm. According to the supervising scientist at the project, one of the prisoners, dissatisfied with the quality of the intricate tools used for the meticulous work, designed his own set of instruments which became "the backbone of our tool kit!"

Sinti Bottle with double serpent engraving

Duck effigy bowl

Bell Plain hunchback effigy bowl

GRACELAND

⟶ 1939 ⟵

*According to the National Park Service, Graceland is "one of the
five most visited home museums in the United States," contributing
around $150 million dollars per year to the Memphis economy.*

Graceland, the home of rock-and-roll legend Elvis Presley, dates from 1939
when Dr. and Mrs. Thomas Moore built the twenty-three-room, Colonial Revival-
style mansion on Highway 51 South (present-day Elvis Presley Boulevard). The
land upon which the house eventually rested was developed by *Memphis Daily
Appeal* publisher, S. E. Toof, who named it Graceland, in honor of his daughter,
Grace. Sometime later, Mrs. Moore, Grace's niece, inherited the property.

In March, 1957, Presley is reported to have paid $102,500 for the house and nearly 100 acres, seeking refuge from his former East Memphis home where issues of his personal privacy and security, along with the growing weariness of neighbors over the endless traffic passing his home, were rapidly developing. Soon afterward, he moved into the house with his father and mother, Vernon and Gladys. Gladys died in 1958, Vernon remarried two years later, and both he and his new wife, Dee Stanley, then lived with Elvis at Graceland. In the meantime, Elvis was drafted, served in the United States Army in Germany, met a beautiful young woman named Priscilla Beaulieu, and moved her into Graceland, where she lived for five years before she and Elvis married in 1967. Five years later, the Presleys separated and eventually divorced. One child, Lisa Marie, was born of the union and in 1985, she sold 85 percent of the estate.

Elvis died at Graceland on August 16, 1977. His impact on popular music and culture is immeasurable. His records, albums, CDs, videos, and movies have been listened to and viewed by people the world over. Today, his popularity remains as high as ever.

Elvis Presley,
"King of Rock 'n Roll"

Graceland is owned and administered by Elvis Presley Enterprises, Inc.

MASON TEMPLE

❖ 1945 ❖

*"Like anybody, I would like to live a long life. Longevity has its place.
But I'm not concerned about that now. I just want to do God's will. And
He's allowed me to go up to the mountain. And I've looked over. And I've
seen the Promised Land. I may not get there with you. But I want you to
know tonight, that we, as a people, will get to the promised land!"*

Dr. Martin Luther King, Jr., April 3, 1968, at Mason Temple

Bishop C. H. Mason's decades-long vision came true in 1945, when the
temple named in his honor was completed in Memphis. Erected at a cost of

❖

$250,000, the massive, three-story structure was built of reinforced concrete, brick, stone, and steel. With a seating capacity of nine thousand, it was the largest assembly hall in the city and the largest African-American-owned church in the United States. Furnished with two cafeterias, two kitchens, a post office, barber and beauty salons, indoor and outdoor sound systems, first aid and emergency health facilities, and more, it was all Bishop Mason had hoped for as a national convocation center and headquarters for his Church of God in Christ.

Dr. Martin Luther King, Jr.

Mason had carried his church far since he organized it and served as its head since the early twentieth century. Gathering places for his church services were many during those early years, but the bishop always maintained that, one day, he would preach from the pulpit of the sanctuary his followers deserved. And, he was not the only one to address eager listeners in the permanent church. Dr. Martin Luther King, Jr., addressed the congregation on April 3, 1968, the day before his assassination.

Since Dr. King's death, Mason Temple has become an official historic site of the civil rights movement. President Bill Clinton and Vice president Al Gore have made racial unity speeches there, and it has hosted many gospel music luminaries.

Mason Temple is the world headquarters for the Church of God in Christ and continues to hold regular services.

LORRAINE MOTEL

SHELBY COUNTY

—— *1925* ——

THE NATIONAL CIVIL RIGHTS MUSEUM

—— *1991* ——

When a single rifle shot disrupted the quiet evening of April 4, 1968, and mortally wounded Dr. Martin Luther King, Jr., on the balcony of his Memphis motel, a new era of civil rights issues was begun.

When Dr. Martin Luther King, Jr., arrived in Memphis in April 1968 to support a strike by the city's 1,300 sanitation workers, he stayed at the Lorraine Motel, primarily because it was an historic part of the South Main district often visited by such black celebrities as Cab Calloway, Aretha Franklin, Nat King Cole, and Roy Campanella. Originally built as a white hotel in 1925, the business had catered almost exclusively to black guests since the end of World War II as the neighborhood gradually transformed. By 1968, the area consisted of low-income workers, mostly renters living in rapidly deteriorating quarters.

On the evening of April 3, Dr. King gave his famous "I've been to the Mountaintop" speech at Mason Temple and afterward retired to the Lorraine. The following evening at around six o'clock, he stepped onto the balcony outside Room 306 to chat with some people in the parking lot, among them Jesse Jackson and Andrew Young. Suddenly, the report of a single rifle shot was heard and the thirty-nine-year-old King crumpled to the balcony, mortally wounded. He died at St. Joseph's Hospital at 7:05 p.m. By his side were his friends Billy Kyles and Ralph Abernathy.

The Lorraine continued its operation as a motel until 1982, when it was foreclosed. Eventually, the Martin Luther King, Jr. Memorial Foundation acquired the property. Five years later, the National Civil Rights Museum was begun on the site, utilizing the original building, as well as the structure from which the fatal gunshot was fired. Presently, the museum commemorates the entire civil rights movement in the United States.

On April 4, 1968, the dreams of millions of Americans were shattered by a single act of violence.

The Lorraine Motel is administered by the National Civil Rights Museum.

BEALE STREET
SHELBY COUNTY
⟶ late 1800s to late 1960s ⟵

One of the most famous streets in America, vibrant, thumping, and rhythmic Beale Street was the heart of African-American culture and music in the mid-south. It was a colorful paradox where religion, entertainment, and civil rights movements co-existed, and a musician named Handy sent the blues out to the world.

New York has its Fifth Avenue, New Orleans has its Bourbon Street, and Chicago has its Wabash Avenue. To African-American Memphians, however, Beale Street is *the* thoroughfare. Like many large Southern towns, the Beale Street neighborhood was originally inhabited by white European immigrants—

merchants, store owners, and craftsmen. Following the Civil War and more stringent segregation laws, the black population of the city nearly tripled and accounted for well over one-half of the population, with many of the new arrivals settling in the area south of Beale Street. By the 1880s, the upper-middle-class, white neighborhood had transformed into a predominately commercial avenue for African Americans. A leader in the transformation was Robert R. Church Sr. (1839–1912), a freedman who, in 1899, purchased six acres of land in the neighborhood, upon which to create a park and build a two-story, two-thousand-seat auditorium. During the years leading up to World War II, city fathers changed the park's name from Church Park and Auditorium to Beale Avenue Park, but the old name was later resurrected and the park underwent re-development by the city in 1987.

Late 1960s urban renewal projects following the assassination of Dr. Martin Luther King, Jr., destroyed

Saturday night on Beale Street

W. C. Handy statue in Handy Park

Beale Street Baptist Church, founded in the late 1840s, is the oldest continuous African-American congregation in Memphis and is the first brick church in the mid-South built by and for blacks. It is considered the Mother Church of all black Baptist churches in the Memphis area.

many of the original buildings that once lined Beale Street. But, during the one-hundred-year occupation by predominately African Americans, the area developed into one of the most recognized centers for several types of distinctive American music: jazz, blues, rockabilly, gospel, and rock and roll. Until the late 1950s, such legends as B. B. King, Mahalia Jackson, and Chattanooga-born Bessie Smith were frequent performers.

One of the most famous blues men of the era was W. C. Handy (1873–1958), known the world over as the "Father of the Blues." He was born in Florence, Alabama, to recently freed slaves and at age 23, joined a minstrel show, moving about the South and eventually ending up in Memphis, where he and his

Daisy Theatre

band played ditties for political candidates. There, he wrote "Memphis Blues," originally called "Mr. Crump," after the city's infamous political boss, Edward H. "Boss" Crump. In 1914, Handy penned the world-famous "Saint Louis Blues," destined to become one of the outstanding pieces of jazz in all history. "Beale Street Blues" came a little later, followed by "John Henry Blues." Handy was a popular figure on Beale Street during the 1920s and 1930s, playing in one of the many clubs lining the rowdy thoroughfare.

The Beale Street Baptist Church is one of Tennessee's oldest African-American churches. Organized in 1864, the present-day building was begun two years later under the direction of Reverend Morris Henderson (1802–1877). By the time Henderson died, the congregation had reached 2,500 members. The building was visited by former president Ulysses S. Grant in 1880, and the civil rights icon, Ida B. Wells, was a member of the church. Around the turn of the twentieth

century, when city mayor Edward H. Crump protested to the church's pastor, George A. Long, about Long giving permission for activist A. Philip Randolph to use the building for a rally, Long replied, "Christ, not Crump, is my Boss."

"By the turn of the last century, Memphis had become the unofficial capital of both cotton culture and the Black Belt. Beale Street was arguably the cultural heart of the African-American world."

Kenneth T. Jackson, Urban Historian at Columbia University, 2009

The Orpheum Theatre, once billed as the "South's Finest Theatre" and "the classiest theatre outside of New York City," was built on the corner of Beale and Main Streets in 1890 and named the Grand Opera House. Catering to vaudeville performances, the theater became part of the national Orpheum vaudeville chain in 1907 and its name was changed to the Orpheum. Rebuilt on the original site in 1928 at a cost of more than one-and-a-half million dollars, the new Orpheum is twice as large as the original building and features a huge Wurlitzer pipe organ,

The Orpheum Theatre, rebuilt in 1928 on the site of the Grand Opera House, c. 1890, and then billed as the "classiest theatre" outside New York City. The Grand was a part of the Orpheum Circuit of vaudeville shows, but burned in 1923 when a fire broke our during a strip-tease performance by Blossom Seeley.

Beale Street
between 2nd and
3rd, c. 1950s

crystal chandeliers, and gilded moldings. Motion pictures came to the Orpheum in 1940, and the theater served as a movie house until 1976. It was purchased the following year by the Memphis Development Foundation and became a venue for Broadway plays and concerts. Between late 1982 and early 1984, the theater was renovated to its 1928 appearance. Since reopening, it has featured such Broadway plays as *Les Miserables*, *Phantom of the Opera*, and *Cats* and hosted many popular entertainment personalities, including Tony Bennett and Jerry Seinfeld.

Reportedly, the ghost of a little girl named Mary, who was tragically killed by a passing trolley nearby in the 1920s, has attended every performance at the Orpheum wearing a white dress and seated in the same box seat for the past eighty years.

Beale Street
between 2nd and
3rd, c. 1950s

Beale Street and 4th,
c. 1940

Royalty in the Beale Street parade for Cotton Maker's Jubilee, founded by Beale Street dentist R.Q Venson in response to the city's Cotton Carnival, which, for all intents and purposes, was for whites only.

Orchestra leader Ben Branch, who's "Operation Breadbasket Orchestra" played on Beale Street. His band, the Largos, played backup for STAX recording artists. Branch was the last person Dr. Martin Luther King, Jr. spoke to moments prior to his assassination at Memphis' Lorraine Motel.

Early photograph of Beale Street jazz orchestra leader, and noted "Father of the Blues," W. C. Handy

MEMPHIS COTTON EXCHANGE AND RIVERFRONT STEAMBOAT LANDING

SHELBY COUNTY

~ 1873 ~

During the late 1800s, Memphis served as the largest inland cotton market in the world.

The first Europeans to view the area around Memphis were members of the Spanish exploring party led by Hernando de Soto, who in 1541 spied the Mississippi River for the first time. Frenchmen came next, and in 1739, Governor Bienville of Louisiana built Fort Assumption near present-day Crump Park. Memphis was founded in 1819 by Andrew Jackson, James Winchester, and John Overton, upon land lying along the east bank of the Mississippi River, which in turn, was part of a much larger cession which the Chickasaw Indians had relinquished to the United States government the previous year. The town grew slowly at first, but by 1834, when Eastin Morris published his book, *The Tennessee Gazetteer*, he revealed that "it must undoubtedly become the emporium of one of the finest agricultural districts in the western country," and that the surrounding

The stone wharf below Front Street and at the confluence of the Wolf River with the Mississippi was the embarkation point for cotton being shipped from Memphis to worldwide markets.

region was supported by "a light sandy soil well adapted to the growth of cotton, which is there the great staple."

Shortly following Nashville's establishment in 1779–80, John Donelson, one the town's co-founders and the father of Andrew Jackson's future wife, Rachel, produced the first cotton crop in present-day Middle Tennessee. Since the three founders of Memphis—Jackson, Overton, and Winchester—were all large landowners and cotton growers in Middle Tennessee, it is only natural that cotton was one of the first crops tested in the rich bottomlands of the Memphis area.

By the time Andrew Jackson became president of the United States in 1829,

cotton was Tennessee's number one agricultural product, and farmers and plantation owners in present-day West Tennessee were contributing their share. Their success was assisted by the fine facilities offered by Memphis, which grew rapidly into one of the largest inland ports in the country. Steamboats by the scores tied up to the wharf, loading and unloading every imaginable product. One boat, however, the *Sultana*, had a much sadder fate. Just days following the close of the Civil War, the former cotton transport, a medium-sized side-wheeler, was overloaded with paroled Union soldiers being transported from Southern prisoner-of-war camps back to their

northern homes. With standing-room-only on her decks, the *Sultana* strained and groaned and her boilers finally blew up, killing more than 1,500 people in what remains the worst American maritime accident in history.

The exportation of Southern cotton was negatively affected by the Civil War, and, hastened by the demise of the plantation culture and the abolishment of slavery, the crop took a tailspin. By the end of Reconstruction, however, many Southern states, including Tennessee, witnessed a new popularity for cotton.

In 1873, amidst hopes of regulating the exportation of cotton from the river port of Memphis, a number of the city's influential businessmen organized the Cotton Exchange, much along the same lines as similar establishments in New Orleans and New York. Not all residents, however, including the publisher of the *Commercial Appeal*, were enthusiastic about the new venture. In a March 5, 1872, article, the newspaper expressed fears that "a Cotton Exchange might bring to Memphis the gambling system of buying cotton, which flourishes in New York. This means 'futures' would be bought and sold and invariably the planters would be cheated."

The present Cotton Exchange building, located at the corner of Front Street and Union, has been home for the Exchange since its construction in 1914. It is also currently the home of the Cotton Exchange Museum.

A 1907 arch of cotton bales over a Memphis street advertises to the world that "Cotton is King."

Following much discussion, the Cotton Exchange opened in 1873. Most likely as a move to garner support from the *Appeal*, the trading of futures was prohibited and all cotton processed there was sold "on the spot" for the present, going rate. Over the years, the continuing success of the Exchange, assisted by the abundant amount of cotton business handled there from Tennessee and other Southern states, vaulted Memphis into the world's largest inland cotton market, a record it held for many years.

Following the Exchange's establishment, the organization operated out of a one-room office located on the northeast corner of Front and Madison Streets. Within a few years, rented rooms proved insufficient for the large volume of Exchange business, and a building fund was organized to finance a $150,000, four-story structure on Second Street between Madison and Court, which was occupied in

Cotton Carnival float
c. 1937

"Royalty" has always presided over the several days of Cotton Carnival celebrations.

The cotton-laden steamboat Katy-D departing Memphis for New Orleans and ports beyond, c. 1930s

October 1885. By 1909, continued success and growth caused Exchange officials to once again relocate the business, this time to a newly-constructed, nineteen-story skyscraper built upon the site of the previous headquarters. Described by a reporter as "one of the most ornate in the South with an ornamental suspended

*"The commerce that took place here is really interesting.
In the old days of cotton trade, we had to be in close proximity to each
other in order to do business. This whole neighborhood [Front Street,
known as Cotton Row] truly functioned as a neighborhood."*

Calvin Turley, Memphis Cotton Merchant

ceiling, numerous pilasters and a three-story double set of marble and bronze stairs on the east side," this striking building was replaced as Exchange offices in 1924, when new, twelve-story headquarters at the corner of Front Street and Union Avenue were occupied. The Cotton Exchange, as well as a recently opened Cotton Museum depicting the history of the plant's social and economic impact on Memphis and the surrounding region, is housed in the 1924 building.

The Memphis Cotton Exchange Association administers the Memphis Cotton Exchange Museum.

Rippavilla, home of Nathaniel Cheairs IV,
built in 1855 in Spring Hill

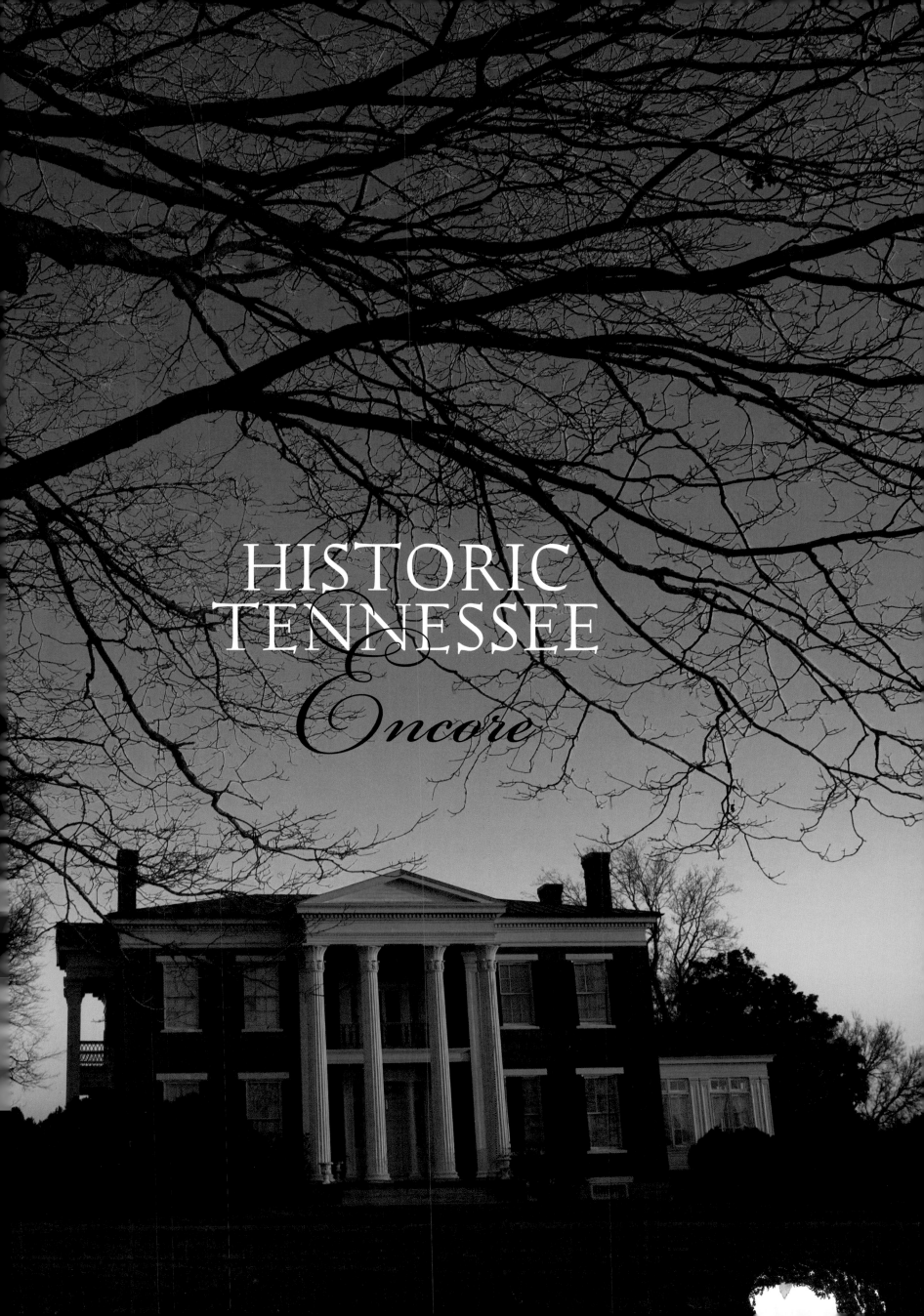

HISTORIC
TENNESSEE

Encore

DOE RIVER COVERED BRIDGE
CARTER COUNTY
1882

The first patent for a covered bridge in the United States was issued in 1797 to Charles Willson Peale, the noted portraitist of George Washington and other eminent Americans. For the next one hundred years or so, hundreds of such bridges were built across the country, particularly in New England and the mid-Atlantic states, but also a fair number in the South. The covered bridge across the Doe River in Elizabethton was built in 1882 at a cost of $3,000 for the bridge, plus an additional $300 for the approaches. The contractor was Dr. E. E. Hunter, who hired Thomas Matson, a railroad engineer, as architect. The truss measures 137 feet long by 16.4 feet wide and contains a single lane for traffic plus a single walkway. The bridge is one of five original covered bridges in Tennessee.

DOAK HOUSE
GREENE COUNTY
1830

The Reverend Samuel Doak (1749–1830) first built on the property upon which this house is located around 1780, when he constructed three log cab-

ins, one each for his home, his church, and his school. Doak, a Presbyterian, was the first of the denomination to preach in present-day Tennessee. In 1818, Doak and his son, Samuel Witherspoon Doak (1785–1864) founded Tusculum Academy, which through a series of mergers eventually became Tusculum College. Taking the mergers into consideration, the school dates its beginnings to 1794 with the formation of Greeneville College by the Reverend Hezekiah Balch and is the oldest college in the state and the twenty-third oldest still in operation in the nation. The Doak House was built in 1830 by the younger Doak and was occupied by Doak descendants until 1970, when the property was donated to Tusculum College. Today, it serves as the Doak House Museum.

OLD GRAY CEMETERY
KNOX COUNTY
1852

In 1852, thirteen acres of rural pastureland located near present-day downtown Knoxville and purchased two years earlier were dedicated as the Old Gray Cemetery. Forty lots were sold at public auction. Named after James Gray, the British poet who penned "Elegy Written in a Country Churchyard," the cemetery is the resting place for many luminaries, including Governor William "Parson" Brownlow, U. S. postmaster-general Horace Maynard, and artist Lloyd Bransom. Many victims of Knoxville's 1854 cholera epidemic are buried there as well. One of the largest funeral processions ever witnessed in the South occurred during 1912, when former governor Robert Taylor's remains were interred at Old Gray (Taylor's body was later moved to Johnson City).

AYRES HALL – THE UNIVERSITY OF TENNESSEE

KNOX COUNTY

1921

The University of Tennessee dates its beginnings to 1794, when its predecessor, Blount College, was chartered by the government of the Territory of the United States South of the River Ohio (present-day Tennessee). As East Tennessee College, the school moved its campus to its present location in 1826, and, in 1879, the present name was bestowed upon the school. Throughout its early existence in Knoxville, the institution grew rapidly, with much construction focused on "The Hill," a natural prominence overlooking the Tennessee River. In 1921, Ayres Hall, the "trademark" of the University of Tennessee, was constructed on The Hill, and, only recently, has undergone extensive, but historically correct, restoration. Special effort has been made to preserve the original roofing tiles, old millwork, paneled doors, and wood flooring, as well as the original terrazzo floors.

MARBLE SPRINGS

KNOX COUNTY

1797

John Sevier (1745–1815) was born in Virginia, but migrated to Tennessee at a young age. He was active in early settlement affairs in present-day East Tennessee and helped command a unit of the "Overmountain Men" who marched from Sycamore Shoals to Kings Mountain in South Carolina in 1780 during the Revolution to defeat a large American loyalist army under the command of Major Patrick Ferguson. Sevier served from 1784–1788 as the only governor of the "Lost State of Franklin," and when Tennessee attained statehood in 1796, he was elected its first governor, eventually serving for six terms. Sevier called his farm in Knoxville, Marble Springs, so named due to the rose marble deposits and many springs on his property. He was living at the site by 1797.

Marble Springs is owned by the State of Tennessee and administered by the Governor John Sevier Memorial Association, under the direction of the Tennessee Historical Commission.

NATIONAL HISTORIC LANDMARK

FORT LOUDOUN

MONROE COUNTY

1756–57

During late 1756 and early 1757, South Carolina colonial troops built Fort Loudoun near the junction of the Little Tennessee and Tellico Rivers in order to strengthen the British presence and influence among the nearby Cherokee Indian towns. The once-strong friendship between the two peoples eventually broke down and, during the summer of 1760, a large number of Cherokees besieged the fort, demanding its surrender, which occurred on August 7. The British commander Paul Demere accepted the benevolent terms offered by the Cherokee chief Oconostota and, three days later, departed the fort with his 180 troops, 60 women, and several children for the trip back to South Carolina. Once on its way, the British party was attacked by Cherokee warriors who killed twenty-five and took the remainder prisoner. British reprisal was swift. The following year, Colonel James Grant thrust

deep into Cherokee country and his army destroyed fifteen towns, burned fifteen hundred acres of crops, and left five thousand Cherokees homeless. By the end of 1761, the great Cherokee War was finally over.

The site of Fort Loudoun, with its reconstructed structures, is administered by the Tennessee Division of State Parks.

WILEY-BETHLEHEM CHURCH
HAMILTON COUNTY
1887
original church 1835

The original log building at this site served as the first church, school, and meeting house for the community on the Tennessee River known as Ross's Landing. It was in this structure in 1838 that "Chattanooga," a Cherokee word meaning "rock coming to a point" (Lookout Mountain), was chosen as the name for the fledgling town. When the twenty-first century opened, officials at Wiley Memorial United Methodist Church in downtown Chattanooga, believed to be the oldest African-American church in East Tennessee, were faced with a dilemma. With less than twenty regular worshipers, the decision was made to attempt a merger with the less-than-ten-year-old Bethlehem Community Center, which had a much larger congregation. In June 2003, the church was rededicated as the Bethlehem-Wiley United Methodist Church with more than three hundred attendees. Members of the old Wiley Church had worshiped on the site since 1838, and the existing building was constructed in 1887 and first called the St. Mark's Methodist Episcopal Church. Among the church's treasures are an ancient pipe organ and beautifully executed stained glass windows.

BRABSON HOUSE
HAMILTON COUNTY
1857–58

The Brabson House, located at 407 E. Fifth Street in downtown Chattanooga, was built by Reese Bowen Brabson, an attorney who was born in Knox County in 1817. Following graduation from Maryville College and the study of law at Dandridge, Tennessee, Brabson married Sarah Maria Keith in 1844 and settled in Chattanooga in 1845. A member of the newly-formed Whig Party, he supported Zachary Taylor's bid for the presidency, then was elected to the Tennessee General Assembly, followed by a stint in the U.S. House of Representatives. Brabson was a slaveholder, yet pro-Union in his views, eventually refusing to serve in the military of either the Union or the Confederate army. He died of typhoid at his Chattanooga home, called the Brabson House, in 1863 and was buried in the Citizens Cemetery. His residence, although presently bearing little resemblance to the original, still stands.

CONFEDERATE CEMETERY
HAMILTON COUNTY
1867

Chattanooga's Confederate Cemetery, located near the campus of the University of Tennessee – Chattanooga, had its beginning when George W. Gardenhire sold the northern portion of the present-day site to a group of Confederate veterans whose goal was to re-inter the bodies of about 141 of their comrades who had been hastily buried during the Civil War along a flood plain of the nearby Tennessee River. During the next thirty years, the cemetery was managed by an organization jointly overseen by veteran and city trustees. In 1902, following the acquisition of additional land, the massive limestone gate and wrought iron battle flag gate designed by Lawrence Thompson Dickinson were dedicated. By 1992, the cemetery had fallen into serious disrepair and the city of Chattanooga, in cooperation with known descendants of Confederate veterans and with funds raised by local Sons of Confederate Veterans chapters and the Military Order of the Stars and Bars, undertook to restore the site, which was rededicated in 1995.

The Chattanooga Confederate Cemetery is maintained by the N. B. Forrest Camp 3 of the Sons of Confederate Veterans, the A. P. Stewart Chapter of the United Daughters of the Confederacy, and the City of Chattanooga.

THE OLD POST OFFICE AND CUSTOM HOUSE

HAMILTON COUNTY

1893

Following construction that required nearly four years, Chattanooga's massive, four-story, Tennessee-marble-faced Custom House was completed in 1893. Occupying a complete downtown city block, the building is a fine example of Richardsonian-Romanesque architecture. When the structure opened for business, it was occupied by the U. S. Post Office, the Internal Revenue Service, the Custom Surveyor and Commissioner's office, several federal courts, U. S. Signal Corps offices, and facilities for the railway mail clerk. The National Weather

Service maintained an observation deck on the roof. The building has undergone several renovations over the years and has been occupied by other tenants, including the Tennessee Valley Authority and, most recently, the U. S. Bankruptcy Court for the Eastern District of Tennessee and the Office of the U. S. Trustee.

The Old Post Office and Custom House is owned by Custom House Realty Partners, LLC and leased to the U. S. General Services Administration.

SOUTHERN RAILWAY FREIGHT DEPOT

HAMILTON COUNTY

1871

The Freight Depot at 1200 Market Street in Chattanooga is one of only two surviving railroad freight depots in the city, the other being the old Tennessee, Alabama and Georgia Railway building at the corner of Newby and 11th Streets. The freight building was originally constructed in 1871 as an iron foundry, then purchased by the Eastern Kentucky and Georgia Railroad in 1894 for use as a freight depot. In 1901, this railroad was incorporated within the Southern Railway system, hence, the depot being often referred to as the Southern Railway Freight Depot. Following the demise of many railroads in the latter half of the twentieth century, the old depot building fell into disuse before becoming the site of John's Railroad Salvage in the late 1970s. It subsequently underwent a four million dollar renovation to become the first phase of Chattanooga's Warehouse Row project. The depot was placed on the National Register of Historic Places in 1983, at which time the building housed a variety of retail shops and business tenants. In 2005, the certified public accounting firm of Henderson Hutcherson & McCullough, PLLC, purchased the depot and began a renovation program that converted the building into office space. The project was completed in February, 2007, when the firm occupied the space.

HUNTER MANSION
HAMILTON COUNTY
--- *1904* ---

The Hunter Mansion was built in 1904 by an influential insurance broker, Ross Faxon, who hired the Ohio architectural firm of Mead and Garfield to design his palatial, Edwardian-style home. Built upon a bluff overlooking the Tennessee River, the home was purchased in 1920 by Anne Taylor Jones Thomas, the widow of Benjamin F. Thomas, a founder of the world's first company to bottle Coca-Cola. Thomas's nephew, George Thomas Hunter, became the chairman of the board of that company and eventually created the Benwood Foundation, a powerful charitable trust. In 1951, the Benwood Foundation donated the Faxon-Thomas house to the Chattanooga Art Association and, after remodeling and making the space appropriate for a museum, opened the premises to the public in 1952 under the name George Thomas Hunter Gallery of Art, since renamed the Hunter Museum of American Art. The original house still serves as the focus of the vastly expanded facilities.

SEAMOUR SHAVIN HOUSE
HAMILTON COUNTY
--- *1952* ---

The Seamour Shavin House, perched atop Missionary Ridge, is the only building in Tennessee designed by the iconic American architect, Frank Lloyd Wright (1869–1959). During his seventy-year career, Wright, recognized by the American Institute of Architects as "the greatest American architect of all time," designed more than eleven hundred houses, schools, museums, bridges, libraries, and offices, of which 409 are still in use. In 1950, Chattanoogans Seamour and Gerte Shavin commissioned Wright to design their two-thousand-square-foot, Usonian-style home overlooking Chattanooga and the Tennessee River, and two years later, the couple moved into the completed structure. Primary materials used both inside and out were Crab Orchard stone and Louisiana cypress wood. Much of the home's built-in features and furniture were also designed by Wright, who never actually visited the site.

NATIONAL HISTORIC LANDMARK
RHEA COUNTY COURTHOUSE
RHEA COUNTY
--- *1891* ---

No doubt, when the Rhea County Courthouse was completed in 1891, none of the approximately 14,000 residents of the county would have ever believed that the attractive, three-story building would one day be the scene of one of the world's most famous tribunals. On trial was a young local teacher, John Scopes, charged with teaching evolution to his class in defiance of Tennessee law. The case pitted prosecutor William Jennings Bryan, a three-time, unsuccessful candidate for the U. S. presidency and the one-time secretary of state in President Woodrow Wilson's cabinet, against a defense team led by Clarence Darrow, arguably the best criminal lawyer in the United States. Through the hot summer of 1925, the trial, attended by newspaper correspondents and radio broadcasters from all over the world, provided comedic relief as the two giants of the justice system ripped into each other with a vengeance. Scopes was given a small fine, Darrow returned to Chicago, and Bryan died shortly thereafter.

CUMBERLAND HOMESTEAD

CUMBERLAND COUNTY

⟶ 1934-1947 ⟶

TOWER

⟶ 1937-1938 ⟶

The Cumberland Homestead was created by a federal subsistence program to relocate unemployed Americans from overpopulated areas of the country to rural regions and teach them new skills. Initiated by President Franklin D. Roosevelt's New Deal, it was one of five such projects to be located in Tennessee, Alabama, South Carolina, Mississippi, and West Virginia. Only the projects in Tennessee and West Virginia were completed before the program was terminated in 1947. Homestead was situated on 10,000 acres of Cumberland Plateau land south of Crossville. All of the buildings, including the residences, were built of local Crab Orchard stone. Anyone in the United States could apply to participate in the home purchase program, but only a small percent qualified. Roads, fences, schools, barns, an administrative building, and the uniquely designed water tower were all constructed by the formerly unemployed men and women who were accepted. In all, more than two hundred homes were built. In terms of total area, the Cumberland Homesteads is the largest National Register District in Tennessee.

The original Homestead administrative building and tower, along with a restored home, are part of the Cumberland Homesteads National Historic District and are administered by the Cumberland Homesteads Tower Association.

BEERSHEBA SPRINGS INN

GRUNDY COUNTY

⟶ 1857 ⟶

The Beersheba Springs Inn and its namesake town took their names from Beersheba Porter Cain, a woman from nearby McMinnville who first discovered the numerous mineral springs in the area in 1833. The inn reached its final majestic proportions shortly before the Civil War when Colonel John Armfield, a Louisiana planter and slave trader, greatly enlarged several adjoining log structures on his property. The form of the Greek Revival building was a rectangle, with rooms situated on all four sides and a large courtyard in the middle that served for outdoor meetings and activities. Serving first as an elegant resort hotel primarily for guests from Louisiana attempting to escape summer's heat, the Inn was purchased by the Methodist Church (present-day United Methodist Church) in 1941 and converted to an assembly center and summer resort. One of Tennessee's first published female writers, Mary Noailles Murfree (1850–1922)—who, in order to get published in a men's publishing world used the pen name, Charles Egbert Craddock—credited Beersheba Springs with the inspiration for several of her highly successful novels written between 1878 and 1914, including *In the Tennessee Mountains* and *In the Clouds*.

UNIVERSITY OF THE SOUTH AT SEWANEE

FRANKLIN COUNTY

1857

On July 4, 1857, several Episcopalian churchmen gathered atop Lookout Mountain near Chattanooga to discuss the creation of a great institution of learning that would become the University of the South at Sewanee. Led by Bishops Leonidas Polk of Louisiana and James Hervey Otey of Tennessee, plans for the university progressed rapidly, and by August 1859, despite the financial Panic of 1857, nearly $500,000 in cash, bonds, and notes had been contributed, as well as gifts of books from Oxford University. Active construction of various buildings began soon afterward. Situated at an altitude of around two thousand feet, the massive campus, called the "Domain," spreads across ten thousand acres of primarily hardwood forest. An 1896 alumnus poignantly described the setting when he wrote,

A towered city set within a wood,
Far from the world, upon a mountain's crest;
Where the storms of life burst not, nor cares intrude.
There Learning dwells and Peace is Wisdom's guest."

The Collegiate Gothic architecture of many of the academic buildings presently on campus, most of them dating to the post-Civil War era, reflects influences from Oxford and other English institutions. When installed in 1958, the fifty-six bells of the Leonidas Polk Memorial Carillon became the third largest such set of chimes in the world. The university presently enrolls around 1,600 students annually.

FALLS MILL

FRANKLIN COUNTY

1873

Falls Mill's utility to its community of Belvidere, Tennessee, began in 1873 when the structure opened as a cotton and wool factory. Converting later to a cotton gin, it was finally operated as a grist mill. Situated on Factory Creek, the handsome frame building is powered by one of the largest waterwheels in the United States, measuring thirty-two feet in diameter. The wheel is a classic example of an overshot wheel, which receives the running water from the millrace *above* the wheel, allowing gravity's flow to turn the wheel. An undershot wheel performs in the opposite direction, receiving water under the wheel, allowing the water to turn the wheel via velocity as opposed to gravity.

Falls Mill is privately owned and operated as a mill, bed and breakfast, and country store.

NATIONAL HISTORIC LANDMARK

WYNNEWOOD

SUMNER COUNTY

c. 1828

Wynnewood, located in Castalian Springs near the site of Bledsoe's Lick, was built by Colonel A. R. Wynne, Stephen Roberts, and William Cage as a stagecoach inn and hostelry along the Nashville-Knoxville road. When Wynne later acquired his partners' interests in the building, he and his family occupied it as a residence until his death in 1893. His grandson, George Wynne, owned the house until the State of Tennessee purchased it in the 1970s and opened it as an historic site. The structure is the largest existing log building in Tennessee, many of the logs measuring twenty feet long, and a few up to thirty-two feet in length. Nearby are the sites of Bledsoe's Station, an early 1780s fort built by Revolutionary War veteran and long hunter Isaac Bledsoe for defense against the Indians, and the hollow sycamore tree in which long hunter Thomas Sharp (Bigfoot) Spencer spent an entire winter during the late 1770s. A killer tornado ripped through the Castalian Springs neighborhood in 2008 and partially destroyed Wynnewood, which is currently undergoing restoration.

Wynnewood is owned by the State of Tennessee and administered by the Bledsoe's Lick Historical Association under the direction of the Tennessee Historical Commission.

ROSEMONT
SUMNER COUNTY
✦ *1828–1834* ✦

Tradition has it that Judge Josephus Conn Guild (1802–1883) and his wife, Katherine Blackmore Guild, resided in a modest "office" built on their five-hundred-acre, thoroughbred horse and longhorn cattle farm near Gallatin while their plantation house was under construction. Guild designed his house, to be called Rosemont, in a fashion unlike many other Middle Tennessee structures of the times. Strongly influenced by New Orleans and Creole architecture, he incorporated many essentials of this style into his home, as well as many Palladian techniques. Guild, in addition to his judicial career, was well-regarded as an

historian and penned the classic book, *Old Times in Tennessee*, published in Nashville in 1878. Upon the judge's death in 1883, Rosemont was subdivided, with the main house and several acres being passed on to various family members, the last of whom, Joan Brown Guild, eventually sold the house and remaining six acres.

Rosemont is owned and administered by the Rosemont Restoration Foundation.

READYVILLE MILL
CANNON COUNTY
✦ *1870s* ✦

In 1797, Charles Ready, a Marylander, migrated to Middle Tennessee by way of North Carolina. Soon, he established his homestead and grist mill along the East Fork of the Stones River near present-day Readyville, on property that became part of Rutherford County in 1804, then Cannon County in 1836. When the county seat moved from Jefferson in 1811, Ready, one of the county's founders, attempted to have Readyville named the new county seat, but Murfreesboro was selected instead. Ready built the first mill on the site in 1812. A few years following its destruction during the Civil War, his daughter and son-in-law erected the existing mill, which remains operational today, following a recent renovation. Standing four stories high and constructed of tulip poplar and oak, it is an imposing sight made all the more interesting by the nearby presence of Ready's original three-story house built in 1829 (located across the river in Rutherford County), as well as a granary, a miller's cabin, and an ice house located adjacent to the mill.

RUTHERFORD COUNTY COURTHOUSE

RUTHERFORD COUNTY

→ *1859* →

The Rutherford County Courthouse is one of only six surviving courthouses in Tennessee built prior to the Civil War (the others are Carter, Dickson, Hawkins, Jefferson, and Williamson Counties). Located on Murfreesboro's town square, the existing building is the third such structure located on the site and was built at a cost of $50,000. During the Federal occupation of Murfreesboro in 1862, Confederate General Nathan Bedford Forrest and his command made a daring raid on the town, capturing the Union garrison, twelve hundred prisoners, and $250,000 worth of war materiel.

CLOVER BOTTOM MANSION

DAVIDSON COUNTY

→ *c. 1853* →

This stately mansion occupies some of Nashville's most hallowed ground. In 1780, the historic farmlands along the banks of the nearby Stones River were the site of the first corn and cotton crops grown by white settlers in Middle Tennessee. The region attained later fame as a horse-racing venue, frequented by Andrew Jackson and other early gentry, as well as the location of a boat-building yard and general store owned by Jackson. Constructed as an imposing Greek Revival home, it was rebuilt inside the original brick walls in the grand Italianate style after a devastating fire in 1859. The home was built by Dr. James Hoggatt and his wife, Mary Ann Saunders Hoggatt, half-sister to Andrew Jackson Donelson. John McCline, born on the property around 1850, provides a moving account of his youth and escape from the plantation in his autobiography, *Slavery in the Clover Bottoms*. Subsequent owners included the Prices and the Stanford brothers, A. F. and R. D., during the early twentieth century. The home was last privately owned by Mrs. Merle Stanford Davis, widow of A. F., who sold it to the State of Tennessee in 1948. The home was used in succeeding years as a state trooper outpost and later converted into apartments for the Tennessee School for the Blind. Since 1994, the home has been the headquarters of the Tennessee Historical Commission, the State Historic Preservation Office.

Clover Bottom Mansion is owned by the State of Tennessee and is managed by the Department of General Services.

MOUNT OLIVET CEMETERY

DAVIDSON COUNTY

→ *1856* →

Nashville's Mount Olivet Cemetery is the third oldest public burial grounds in the city. Located on 250 acres of land lying along the Lebanon Pike, it was organized in 1856, following Spring Hill Cemetery (1785) on the Gallatin Pike and the Old City Cemetery (1822) on Fourth Avenue South. The old gatehouse to the cemetery (now demolished) was once manned by an armed guard who defiantly questioned each and every would-be visitor to determine if he or she really had business there. Many curiosity seekers were turned away by the guard who took his position seriously. Among Mount Olivet's more historic features is Confederate Circle, wherein approximately 1,500 Confederate soldiers and veterans from all over the region are interred. Some of Nashville's most prominent and influential citizens are buried here, among them, Adelicia Acklen, mistress of Belmont Mansion; Captain Thomas Ryman, builder of the Ryman Auditorium as a house of worship; David Lipscomb, founder of Lipscomb University; John Catron, the first Tennessean appointed to the United States Supreme Court; John Overton, Jr., builder of the Maxwell House Hotel; Confederate General Benjamin Franklin Cheatham; and Speaker of the U. S. House of Representatives Joseph W. Byrns, whose funeral President Franklin D. Roosevelt attended in 1936.

GLEN LEVEN
DAVIDSON COUNTY
—— *1857* ——

The history of the beautiful Nashville home known as Glen Leven extends far beyond the existing house built just prior to the Civil War by John Thompson. Sited on a land grant owned by John's ancestor, Thomas Thompson, a signer of the Cumberland Compact, it was preceded by a frontier station, or fort, constructed during Nashville's earliest days and known as Thompson's Station. It was from this property that young Alice Thompson was kidnapped by Creek Indians in 1792, but released two years later. In the Civil War, during the Battle of Nashville, Glen Leven was caught between the Union and Confederate lines along the Franklin Pike, but remarkably escaped harm and served as a Union hospital. Glen Leven has recently been acquired from the last of the Thompson family, Susan M. West, by the Land Trust of Tennessee, under whose administration it presently operates.

NATIONAL HISTORIC LANDMARK
PEABODY COLLEGE
DAVIDSON COUNTY
—— *1875* ——

Peabody College had its origins in 1875 when the University of Nashville divided into two separate entities: a prep school called the University School of Nashville, and George Peabody College for Teachers. From around 1911, Peabody's campus was located on 21st Avenue South in Nashville, directly across the street from Vanderbilt University's campus. The site was originally occupied by an early African-American college, Roger Williams University. Peabody and Vanderbilt shared students, classes, and library facilities until 1979, when Peabody, suffering from economic problems, was merged with Vanderbilt. The school's twenty-two primary buildings and its fifty-acre campus are presently known as the Peabody College of Education and Human Development at Vanderbilt University.

NASHVILLE UNION STATION
DAVIDSON COUNTY
—— *1900* ——

Union Station in Nashville is one of America's finest examples of Richardsonian-Romanesque design.

Work began on the massive stone structure in 1898, requiring two years to complete. Built as the hub of the Louisville and Nashville Railroad (L. & N.), but servicing the Nashville, Chattanooga, and St. Louis Railway (N. C. & St. L.) as well, the building's vaulted lobby reaches a height of sixty-five feet and is highlighted with stained glass, a huge limestone fireplace, marble floors, gold-leaf medallions, and a series of *bas-relief* panels. When the facility was dedicated in 1900, it housed two alligator ponds on the track level, and a train shed, the largest unsupported structure in the United States at the time, capable of simultaneously housing ten multi-car trains. As more speedy forms of transportation overtook railroads as the country's favorite form of travel, Union Station fell into disrepair. In 1986, it was restored, totally renovated, and rededicated as a luxury hotel. Today, it is owned and operated as a Wyndham Historic Hotel.

MEETING OF THE WATERS
WILLIAMSON COUNTY
1809

The architectural genius from whose ideas sprang the classic Georgian style of building design that was so popular in England and America in the eighteenth and early nineteenth centuries would have felt totally at home in the Forest Home community of Williamson County. There, within a few miles of each other, stood the magnificent houses of the Perkins family, the oldest of which was Meeting of the Waters, named because of its placement at the confluence of the West Harpeth and Harpeth Rivers. Its builder, Thomas Hardin Perkins, born in 1757 in Halifax County, Virginia, was an officer in the American Revolution and had been awarded a large amount of land in Middle Tennessee for his services. When he arrived in Williamson County around 1800, he began work on his home, a decade-long effort. Upon the death of Perkins in 1838, Meeting

of the Waters was inherited by his daughter, Mary Hardin Perkins, and her husband and cousin, Nicholas "Bigbee" Perkins, builder of nearby Montpier, another significant example of the Federal style from early Tennessee.

ST. PAUL'S EPISCOPAL CHURCH
WILLIAMSON COUNTY
1834

St. Paul's Episcopal Church is housed in the oldest existing church building in Franklin. Organized in 1827, it also serves the oldest Episcopal congregation in Tennessee, and the structure is the oldest Episcopal church building in continual use in the United States, west of the Appalachian Mountains. In 1821, James Hervey Otey (1800–1863) arrived in Franklin and founded Harpeth Academy. He was soon ordained a priest in the Episcopal Church and gradually assumed more responsibility until 1833, when he was appointed Bishop of Tennessee. Otey served as rector at St. Paul's until 1835, when he moved to nearby Columbia to fulfill his bishopric duties. During the Civil War, St. Paul's sanctuary was used as a barracks, horse stable, and hospital by Union troops, resulting in a great deal of interior damage. Following hostilities, a major remodeling effort was begun, resulting in essentially the plan that is visible today. In early 1912, nearly fifty years after the war's end, the United States government finally reimbursed officials of several Franklin churches, including St. Paul's, for the damages inflicted upon their buildings. St. Paul's rector was awarded $2,450, more than any of the other recipients.

HARRISON HOUSE

WILLIAMSON COUNTY

c. 1848

In his diary for 1848, Dr. Samuel Henderson, a distinguished Franklin physician, recorded that a certain "Mr. Harrison" was "well-to-do" and resided in "a fine home on Columbia Pike." The home's owner, William Harrison, Sr., had served as Williamson County's sheriff from 1836 to 1842, having migrated from Virginia to the Franklin area some years earlier. The exact date of the completion of his imposing, Greek Revival-style home, present-day Harrison House, is unknown, but was obviously some time prior to the diary entry. Aside from its architectural beauty, the Harrison House possesses additional significance. In early September 1864, Confederate General John H. Kelly was killed nearby during skirmishing with Union troops and was buried on the grounds, before being re-interred in Mobile in 1866. During the hours leading up to the Battle of Franklin on November 30, 1864, Confederate General John Bell Hood utilized the house as his command post and in a breakfast meeting with his senior staff, including General Nathan Bedford Forrest, he made the fateful decision to attack the Union-held town. Less than eight hours later, Franklin was lost to the Confederacy, Hood's Army of Tennessee was decimated, and the Union army was on its way to defend Nashville.

> "The oldest homes sit so right on the land. They're part of the history and legacy of the place, as rooted in the soil as the grasses and trees."
>
> Barry Parker, in *Williamson County: The Land and Its Legacy*, 2001

NATIONAL HISTORIC LANDMARK

MONTGOMERY BELL TUNNEL

CHEATHAM COUNTY

1818

Montgomery Bell (1769–1855), an early Middle Tennessee ironmaster originally from Pennsylvania, speculated in several iron-bearing properties along the western Highland Rim. In order to process the iron ore from his nearby mines, Bell built the Patterson Forge along the Harpeth River. For power, he had his slaves dig a 290-foot-long tunnel through a high ridge separating the river in a narrow horseshoe bend where the two parts of the stream were less than 300 feet apart, even though the river distance between the two points was seven miles. The vertical difference between the entrance to the tunnel and its exit was several feet, allowing power to be generated at the exit end by the rushing waters. The tunnel was the first of its type in the United States, and several years later, the forge's facilities were considered as a potential site for a national armory.

Montgomery Bell Tunnel and the Patterson Forge are part of the Harpeth River State Park.

RIPPAVILLA

MAURY COUNTY

1855

For three long years, Rippavilla's walls were raised out of the ground and on three separate occa-

CHERRY MANSION
HARDIN COUNTY
c. 1830

Sometime around 1830, upon the site of an earlier house constructed by James Rudd who operated the ferry across the Tennessee River, David Robinson built his Georgian style home, Cherry Mansion. Situated on a high bluff above the river, the house witnessed quite a bit of Civil War action, not the least of which was its occupation by Union General Ulysses S. Grant for a period of six months prior to the battle at Shiloh in April 1862. The mansion's hostess at the time was Annie Irwin Cherry, daughter of the builder, and she later wrote of Grant's reaction when he received the news that the battle had begun. "He was at my breakfast table when he heard the report of a cannon, holding untasted a cup of coffee; he paused in conversation to listen, then hastily arose, saying to his staff officers, 'Gentlemen, the ball is in motion, let's be off.' His flagship was lying at the wharf, and in fifteen minutes, he, his staff officers, orderlies, clerks, and horses had embarked for the battlefield." Two other Union generals, C. F. Smith and W. H. L. Wallace, died at Cherry Mansion, the latter from wounds suffered at Shiloh.

CAPITOL THEATRE
OBION COUNTY
1927

At seven o'clock on the evening of April 11, 1927, the Capitol Theatre in Union City had its grand opening before a packed house of 825 moviegoers who paid twenty-five cents for an adult ticket, or ten cents for a child's admission. The theater's management promised only "carefully selected pictures, that could offend no one, yet that can delight and entertain the most particular people." The evening's performance was *Knockout Riley*, starring Richard Dix. Built and owned by the Crescent Amusement Company, the Capitol was one of many movie houses across the South overseen by Crescent's legendary Tony Sudekum. As downtown business diminished in Union City, other theaters opened on the town's outskirts, taking away a large portion of the Capitol's badly needed revenues. The old movie house closed its doors on August 15, 1991, with a performance of *Boys N the Hood*. In 1994, following an extensive renovation, the Capitol Theatre was acquired by a group of interested citizens who produce live performances under the name, the Masquerade Theatre.

"The evolution of the plantation culture of the lower Mississippi valley…
during the early and middle years of the nineteenth century, put forth an
architectural efflorescence amazing both for its vigor and its feeling for materials."

Clarence John Laughlin, in *Ghosts Along the Mississippi*, 1948

"Such symbols [of our heritage]
preserved by a longing tethered to the past,
whether it be a distant church spire, a gracious bend in an old road
or just a reverence for trees and the old ways of farm life,
become more important as they vanish."

Eric Sloane, in *Our Vanishing Landscape*, 1955

THE PILLARS
HARDEMAN COUNTY
c. *1826*

John Houston Bills (1800–1871), a founder of
Bolivar, Tennessee, and a leading businessman, cotton factor, and political figure in the area, purchased
The Pillars in 1837 and since then the home has
been visited by many state and national dignitaries,
including Jefferson Davis, Andrew Jackson, and
David Crockett. The Pillars is a unique early asymmetrical design representing a plantation house
typology development common to important houses
before the advent of Anglo-influenced symmetrical
designs. This arrangement was common in the
Caribbean from the 1500s and Mississippi River
Valley from the early 1700s as it spread up the
Natchez Trace and into Tennessee. It is an important and significant early architectural style that
harkens to an even earlier form, a process and style
referred to as *retardataire* architecture.

**The Pillars is owned and operated by the
Hardeman County Chapter of the Association for
the Preservation of Tennessee Antiquities.**

TRINITY IN THE FIELDS CHAPEL
TIPTON COUNTY
1847

Nestled among a grove of ancient red cedar
trees, themselves surrounded by a sea of cotton fields
between the towns of Mason and Charleston, rests
Trinity in the Fields Episcopal Chapel. The structure
was built in 1847, replacing an earlier sanctuary, St.
Andrews, which dated from 1834 but was destroyed
by fire eleven years later. The land upon which the
chapel was built was a gift from a local plantation
owner, Major William Taylor. Reverend James W.
Rogers served as the chapel's first rector. Trinity
Chapel's proximity to Mason, founded in the mid-
1850s, placed the church near the Memphis and
Ohio Railroad, a major north-south communications
link during the Civil War. Abraham Lincoln's foe
and United States presidential candidate, Stephen A.
Douglas, as well as Confederate States of America
President Jefferson Davis, visited the area, the former
in 1860 and the latter during the war.

ELMWOOD CEMETERY
SHELBY COUNTY
— 1852 —

In 1852, fifty Memphis citizens banded together, each contributing $500, and organized Elmwood Cemetery, the oldest active burial ground in Memphis. The $25,000 the group raised purchased forty acres of land two miles southeast of the city. Less than one year later, the cemetery received its first interment, Mary Berry. The original plot was eventually augmented by another forty acres and, in time, the whole was surrounded by homes and buildings of a rapidly expanding Memphis. The office, a Carpenter Gothic cottage, was built in 1866, and, since the 1870s, its bell has tolled the arrival of every funeral procession. Nineteen Confederate generals have reposed in the cemetery, including Nathan Bedford Forrest, whose body was later removed to Forrest Park. Other notable Memphians buried in Elmwood include Andrew Jackson Donelson; Edward H. "Boss" Crump; Senator Kenneth McKellar; the "Mother of Beale Street," Lillie Mae Glover; renowned Civil War historian, Shelby Foote; and scores of victims of the *Sultana* disaster of 1865.

ST. PETER CATHOLIC CHURCH
SHELBY COUNTY
— 1852–1855 —

Although the existing St. Peter Church building in Memphis was completed between 1852 and 1855, the parish it serves dates from 1840 and is the oldest Roman Catholic congregation in West Tennessee. The first church structure on the site measured only thirty by seventy feet and was completed in 1842 at a cost of $5,000. Four years later, the Dominican Order inherited the administration of the parish and continues its oversight today. The present sanctuary was devised by a leading church architect of the period, Patrick Charles Keely, and his use of vaulted ceilings, stained glass windows, upward thrusting arches, and vertical clustered piers are all in keeping with the Norman Gothic design. Eight priests and eleven sisters of St. Peter perished during the yellow fever and cholera epidemics that struck Memphis during the 1870s. The church was extensively renovated in 1982.

PINK PALACE MANSION
SHELBY COUNTY
— 1923 —

The Pink Palace, so named because of its exterior finishing of pink Georgian marble, was built in 1923 by Memphis entrepreneur and pioneering grocer Clarence Saunders. The twenty-two-room mansion—complete with a ballroom, indoor shooting range, and what is presently known as a media room—made quite a splash in the local news, especially since Saunders had come from such humble beginnings. He had arrived in Memphis in 1904, peddling groceries for a wholesaler, but within a dozen years, he had organized what became the giant Piggly Wiggly grocery chain, the nation's first self-service, super market. Saunders opened his first store at 79 Jefferson Street in Memphis, and before he was through, more than 2,500 Piggly Wigglys covered the entire nation. Sadly, Saunders lost his entire fortune—and his beloved Pink Palace —during severe financial reverses in the 1920s. In 1930, the property was purchased by the Memphis Museum of Natural History and Industrial Arts and, over the years, converted into a state-of-the-art historical and science museum. Especially striking is the large, three-panel mural depicting the history of Memphis, painted by Works Progress Administration artist Burton Callicott.

The Pink Palace Mansion, along with the Mallory-Neely House and the Magevney House, is part of the Pink Palace Family of Museums.

RHODES COLLEGE
SHELBY COUNTY
→ *1925 as Southwestern* ←

Although Rhodes College has been called by its present name only since 1984, the school traces its origin to 1848, when the Masonic University of Tennessee opened in Clarksville, Tennessee. After several name changes and its move to Memphis in 1925, it became known as Southwestern, then Southwestern at Memphis, and finally Rhodes. Its name is in honor of Peyton Nalle Rhodes, a former president of the institution. Situated upon a one-hundred-acre campus near the Memphis Zoo and Overton Park, the Rhodes infrastructure consists of several Collegiate Gothic-style structures, among them Palmer Hall, Robb and White Dormitories, and Kennedy Hall, all original buildings dating from 1925. Henry Hibbs and Charles Klauder designed the original buildings, and later additions, including

the Catherine Burrow Refectory in 1957 and Halliburton Tower in 1962, were designed by H. Clinton Parrent, an associate. The newest addition to the campus is the Paul Barret Jr. Library.

NATIONAL HISTORIC LANDMARK

SUN STUDIO
SHELBY COUNTY
→ 1952 ←

Perhaps the finest compliment the Sun Records label ever received was the quotation that reads, "If music was a religion, then Memphis would be Jerusalem and Sun Studio would be its most holy shrine." Indeed, like Jerusalem, Memphis in general and Sun Studio in particular provided the birthplace for a movement that took on the world, and, once it began, has never diminished in popularity. Rock-and-roll was born here in the early 1950s, pioneered by such artists as Elvis Presley, Jerry Lee Lewis, Roy Orbison, and Carl Perkins. But, before rock-and-roll, there was rhythm-and -blues with its own performers, B.B. King, Ike Turner, and others. Both music movements and practically every early artist involved in them were either discovered or received gargantuan boosts to their careers by Sam Phillips (1923–2003) at his Sun Studio located at 706 Union Street in downtown Memphis.

*"How will we live without our lives?
How will we know it's us without our past?"*

John Steinbeck, in *The Grapes of Wrath*, 1939

Andrew Jackson's kitchen at the first Hermitage, built in 1806, in which slaves lived and prepared meals.

"It isn't too late to still see many of these old structures that link us to our frontier heritage. But...the day is shortly coming when our country will be typically modern, with none of the remembrances of the old days left."

James A. Crutchfield, in *The Harpeth River: A Biography*, 1972

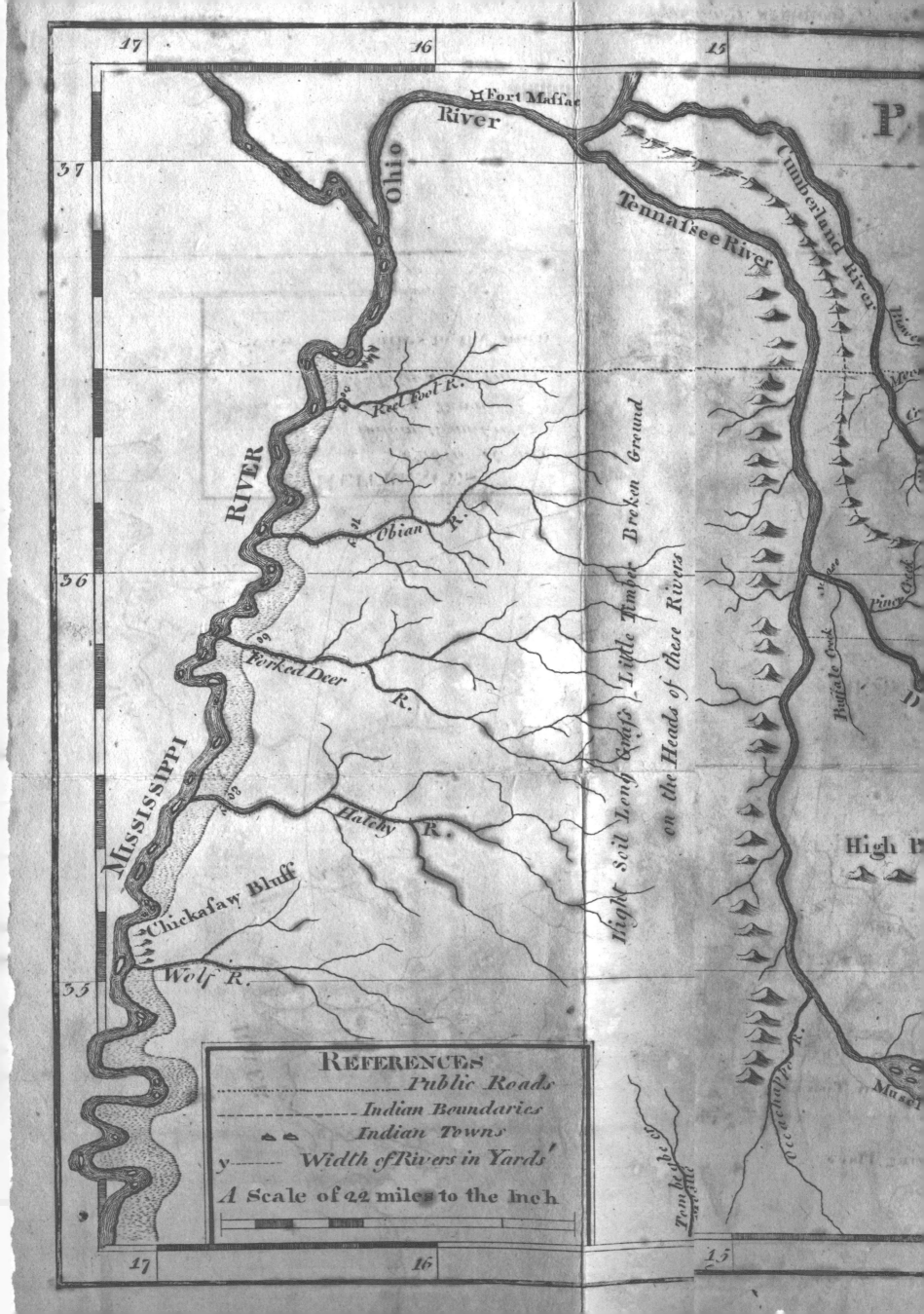

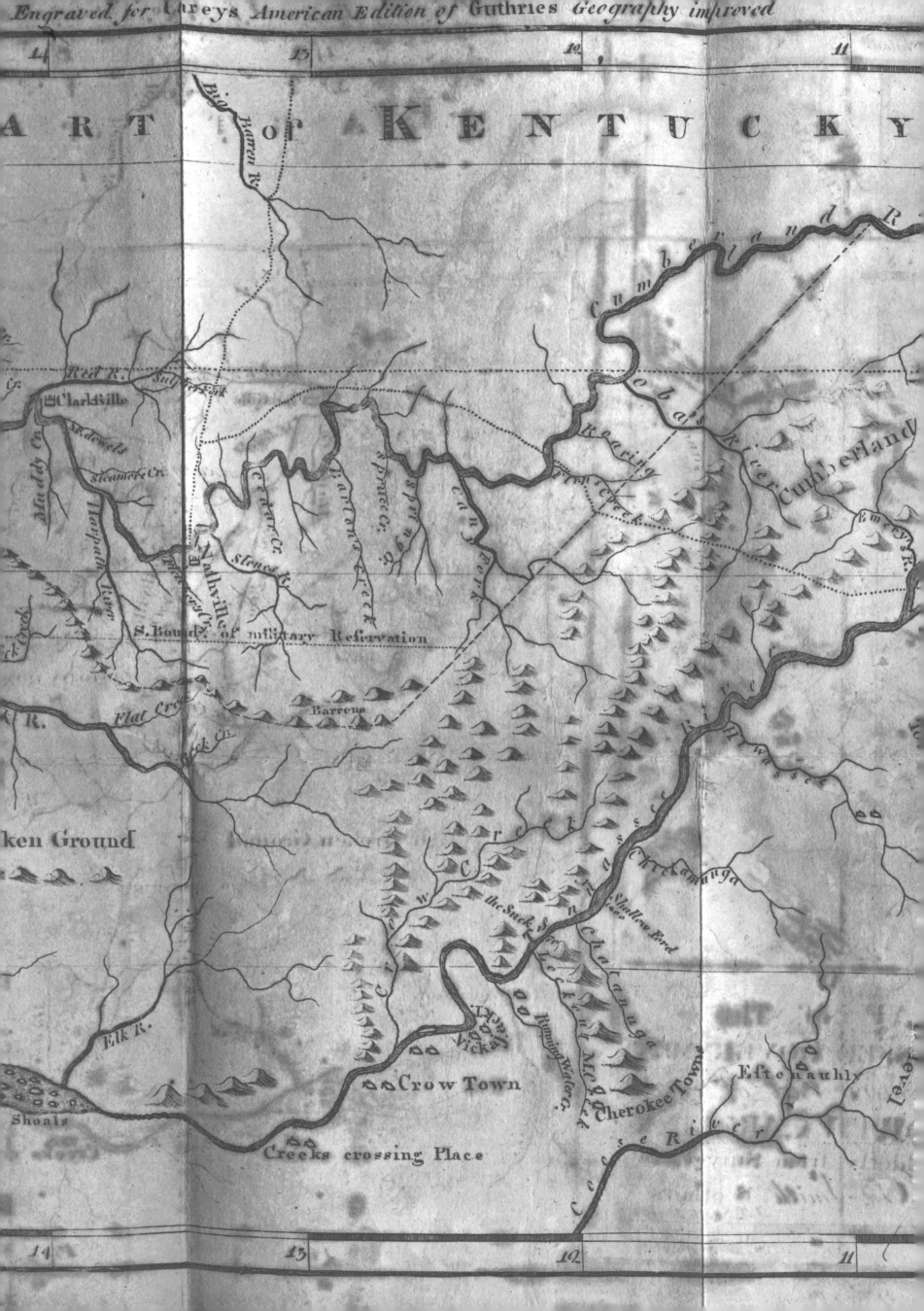